Praise for *Open Heritage Data: An introduction to research, publishing and programming with open data in the heritage sector*

'Digitisation in Galleries, Libraries, Archives and Museums is becoming more prevalent, and so is sharing the data that results from that effort in open and reusable forms. However, navigating the complex information environment to identify, locate, reuse and repurpose openly licensed heritage data can be tricky. In this useful introductory text, Roued-Cunliffe covers a wealth of issues regarding openly available digitised content, including legal, technical and social aspects. Covering use, users, methodological approaches and infrastructure, this is a timely compass to those considering how open data fits into their research – or art – practices, showing the range of activities that can be possible once collections allow reuse and repurposing of their digital assets.'
Melissa Terras, Professor of Digital Cultural Heritage, University of Edinburgh

'Open, heritage and data are by no doubt some of the most debated and discussed concepts of our time. In contrast to much of the earlier work that has focused on either the practical or theoretical sides of data and openness in the heritage field, this wonderfully approachable volume provides an insightful and personal introduction to open heritage data both in theory – and through easy-to-start with hands-on exercises in tapping into various types of heritage data – also in practice.'
Isto Huvila, Professor of Information Studies, Uppsala University

'This book offers a unique take on one of the most urgent challenges for the GLAM sector today – that of building bridges between cultural heritage professionals and new technologies. It's a blatant lack in our skillset not to be able to understand the machinery that so shapes how we work with heritage in the 21st century. Roued-Cunliffe to the rescue! With her combined background in archaeology, teaching and coding, she competently guides us through the tech maze, opening up the world of open heritage data both as a philosophy and toolbox in clear, pedagogical steps.'
Merete Sanderhoff, Curator and Senior Advisor, SMK, The National Gallery of Denmark

'Digitisation is not enough. Roued-Cunliffe's book is both a strong argument for the sharing of heritage data, and a font of inspiration and ideas. Mixing discussions of copyright with snippets of code, she encourages institutions and individuals to make a start – to look beyond the problems and explore the potential of open heritage data for creativity and research.'
Tim Sherratt, Associate Professor of Digital Heritage, University of Canberra

T0333904

Open Heritage Data

Every purchase of a Facet book helps to fund CILIP's advocacy, awareness and accreditation programmes for information professionals.

Open Heritage Data

An introduction to research, publishing and programming with open data in the heritage sector

Henriette Roued-Cunliffe

facet
publishing

Published by Facet Publishing
7 Ridgmount Street, London WC1E 7AE
www.facetpublishing.co.uk

Facet Publishing is wholly owned by CILIP:
the Library and Information Association.

British Library Cataloguing in Publication Data
A catalogue record for this book is available from the British Library.

ISBN 978-1-78330-359-5 (paperback)
ISBN 978-1-78330-360-1 (hardback)
ISBN 978-1-78330-361-8 (e-book)

First published 2020

Text printed on FSC accredited material.

Typeset from author's files in 10/13pt Palatino and Open Sans by Flagholme Publishing Services.
Printed and made in Great Britain by CPI Group (UK) Ltd, Croydon, CR0 4YY.

This book is dedicated to my clever and strong daughter, Bess

Contents

List of case studies, figures and tables

Case studies

Figures

Tables

List of abbreviations

3D	three dimensional
AIF	Arab Image Foundation
API	Application Programming Interface
BCE	before Common Era
CC	Creative Commons
CC BY	Creative Commons Attribution
CC NC	Creative Commons NonCommercial
CC ND	Creative Commons NoDerivatives
CC SA	Creative Commons ShareAlike
CC0	Creative Commons Zero
CE	Common Era
CSS	cascading style sheets
CSV	comma-separated values
DC	Dublin Core
DDD	Danish Demographic Database
DF	Dataframe
DFS	Danish Family Search
DIY	do-it-yourself
DPLA	Digital Public Library of America
GDPR	General Data Protection Regulation
GIF	Graphics Interchange Format
GLAM	Galleries, Libraries, Archives and Museums
HTML	Hypertext Markup Language
HTTP	HyperText Transfer Protocol
JS	JavaScript
JSON	JavaScript Object Notation
LOD	Linked Open Data
MARC	MAchine Readable Cataloguing
OCR	optical character recognition
OHD	Open Heritage Data

OL	Open Layers
OSM	Open Street Map
PAS	Portable Antiquities Scheme
PDF	Portable Document Format
PHP	PHP: Hypertext Preprocessor
RDF	Resource Description Framework
SMK	National Gallery of Denmark
SOCH	Swedish Open Cultural Heritage
UNESCO	United Nations Educational, Scientific and Cultural Organization
URL	Uniform Resource Locator
W3C	World Wide Web Consortium
WGS	World Geodetic System
XML	Extensible Markup Language

Acknowledgements

Thank you to everyone who has answered my questions along the way. Thank you to André De Lemos Freixo, Lancashire Online Parish Clerks, Dan Nicolaysen, Milena Popova, Donghee Sinn, Monique Szpak and Lene Wul.

Thank you to my colleagues at the University of Copenhagen; to those who taught me it's okay to say 'no'; to those who supported me during the rough times; to those who showed me that academics don't have to take themselves too seriously; and to those who make working at a university 'hyggelig'.

Thank you to everyone at Facet Publishing, both old and new, for encouraging and enabling this book, and for their support and patience during the process.

Thank you to my mother for teaching me that implementation of digital technology has to be useful, and to my father for teaching me that legal texts aren't scary.

Thank you to Ane and Susanne for helping this book along by reading parts of it and asking sharp and reflective questions. The book is so much better for it.

Thank you to Sue and Jim for your support and massive help with the book. My life is better for knowing that I can always count on you.

Thank you to my husband, John, for the way you keep the world at bay for me. I wouldn't do it without you. Definitely, not without your fish 'n' chips.

Preface

This book has been a long time in the making. My first experience with making heritage more available through the use of digital technology and data was actually rather analogue. In 2002 I spent a year in Hanoi, Vietnam as an au pair for a Danish family. During my free time I volunteered for the Friends of Viet Nam Heritage Project, which aimed to translate the texts and labels in the Museum of Vietnamese History from Vietnamese into French and English. According to a certificate signed by the Director of the Museum (but worded by the project volunteers), I took a widely varied group of translations and codified them in a standard final form for printing for the museum. This sounds quite advanced. In reality, I remember using some version of MS Word to make a numbered diagram of the exhibition case and typed up the translations to match. Nevertheless, it taught me valuable lessons about making digital tools that are useful for their purpose, about the value of including heritage amateurs in the work of institutions, about the importance of sharing heritage data and about not being afraid to work with this digitally.

These lessons have come in handy to me as a student of archaeology, in my work in museums, on excavations and in my research in digital heritage.

When I began to work with open heritage data for my MSc in Archaeological Computing at the University of Southampton, information on data sharing was sparse. I remember the first time I tried to search the web for information on how to implement the Simple Object Access Protocol (SOAP). Having no idea what to search for other than SOAP, I ended up looking at many results for various scented soaps. Coming to this type of coding from a background mainly in the humanities, I had little idea of how to search and find the information I needed in order to get my 'Heritage Portals and Cross-Border Data Interoperability' project to work (Roued Olsen, 2007a). I was not even sure what information I needed. This also seems to be the case for most people I know in heritage – students, professionals and amateurs. We rarely have a computer science background and the learning curve can sometimes be so steep that it becomes an impossible challenge. It is this experience that has motivated me to write this book, and a wish to take the reader by the hand and demonstrate the very basics of working with open data in the heritage field. I hope to make the learning curve a little smoother for beginners – because, as this book will illustrate, working with heritage data in an open manner is important for the future and cannot be left to computer scientists alone.

Henriette Roued-Cunliffe
Copenhagen, 30 October 2019

Introduction

'It is a truth universally acknowledged, that a single man in possession of a good fortune, must be in want of a wife.'

So begins Jane Austen's *Pride and Prejudice* (1813).

'My mom gave each of us one of these last Christmas. I have yet to wear it … ever!'

And so continues Lizzie Bennet, main character of YouTube show *The Lizzie Bennet Diaries* (Su, 2012), holding up a pink T-shirt with the quote across the front and back.

The works of Jane Austen (1775–1817) are a great example of heritage material, in this case 19th-century literature that spans the centuries and continues to spark the creative minds of today. In recent years her works have been revamped and adapted for a variety of new and old media. New adaptations may include zombies (Grahame-Smith and Austen, 2009) or social media (Su, 2012), but they acknowledge that the words Austen wrote at her portable writing desk 200 years ago (Welland, 2008) are still relevant today.

Galleries, libraries, archives and museums (collectively known as GLAM institutions) from around the world are tackling similar questions. Do people still need us? Does anyone care about heritage? Do our activities have any impact on society? This is clearly exemplified by the 2017 *Impact Playbook* by (as they style themselves) Europeana and friends (Verwayen, 2017), and cemented in every conversation I have ever had with heritage professionals. The worry that underlies these questions is often at the forefront of our minds, but the answers are not as simple as we would like them to be. Digitisation and digital media are not the great solutions we once hoped. There is more to it than that, as we shall see throughout this book.

I have been inspired to write this book by the students and heritage professionals who have followed my courses or taken a workshop with me on the theoretical aspects of heritage openness or the practical aspects of working with heritage data. It is always such a joy to watch as people overcome their apprehension of technology and successfully produce a 'Hello World' message on the screen, and then go on to present data in their own way from different sources. Therefore, this book will include practical tutorials alongside case studies and theoretical work so as to give readers an opportunity to test using open heritage data (OHD) on their own. Some of the examples will be more suitable for those with a moderate level of programming experience, but my aim is for even novices to take something away from this and experience the thrill of visualising a heritage dataset of their choice in a simple way. The examples will be based upon open datasets provided through web APIs[1] that are available for anyone to use.

The title of this book is made up of three words that in themselves are relevant concepts for the subject of the book: Open, Data and Heritage. Further, combinations of these three words form three other concepts: Open Heritage, Open Data and Heritage Data. The idea of openness can be found in many different contexts, none more relevant for society than in the idea of Open Government. Here, openness means transparency towards the public as well as engaging with the public to improve society for everyone (Hamilton and Saunderson, 2017, 17). Open Heritage is a part of Open Government, as heritage institutions and professionals in many societies are a part of, and are funded in a large part by, national governments. Thus, the same openness that is required of government at every level is or should also be required of the heritage sector.[2] Other concepts of openness are Open Access, Open Source and Open Data. The former two are a way of making, respectively, research and computer software freely available to all. Open Data enables datasets to be freely available to anyone with an internet connection.

Finally, Heritage Data is a concept that is making its way into the collective consciousness of the heritage sector at large. Heritage is defined by UNESCO as our legacy from the past, what we live with today and what we pass on to future generations (UNESCO, 2008, 5). Heritage data, then, is both the datasets made up of heritage information and information about heritage objects (i.e. metadata). However, most heritage professionals whom I have spoken to are not sure what is meant by heritage data even though they work with it every day when they take photographs, map archaeological excavations and register objects in databases. Different parts of the heritage sector have actively worked with heritage data and datasets for many years, often as a specialised sub-field. This is the case when working with heritage texts, where a small group of researchers may specialise in XML (eXtensible Markup Language) encoding or text mining, while the majority work with historical text or literature in a more traditional manner, but now using text-editing software. We also have fields like archaeology where the use of data management, Geographical Information Systems and various data analysis is becoming the norm rather than a specialist assignment.

Nevertheless, this book aims to inspire and kick-start further engagement with these concepts, but not necessarily all at once. Readers can use the book to understand arguments for Open Heritage or Open Data, or be further inspired to work with Heritage Data or even Open Heritage Data as they see fit.

In parallel with working in the field of digital heritage and examining how GLAM institutions are tackling this, I have also taken a keen interest in the other side of the coin, namely, how heritage amateurs are tackling digital heritage. By heritage amateurs I mean a large group of people worldwide who take a non-professional interest in heritage, in the sense that they have not been educated in it, nor are they paid to do it. These should not be confused with museum or archive volunteers. Instead they are interest driven and usually participate in heritage in their leisure time, often outside of institutions. This will be explored further in Chapter 1 through examples and selected cases. Most heritage work begins with amateurs and then moves into the professional sphere. Chapter 1 will explore this process and show how the history of the heritage sector is one of opening up to more people through different ways of recording, storing and disseminating heritage material. Open data is presented as one such step towards opening up heritage and heritage collections to more people and for more creative uses. The chapter also presents the Open Heritage Data Model, through five questions that can be used to discuss the level of openness in online collections.

On top of the concern about whether the heritage sector has enough societal impact, I have observed much anxiety about the legal aspects of sharing heritage data online. A couple of years ago copyright was the main question on everyone's lips. Who has the right to publish a material? 'Did you hear about the archive that got sued by the photographer's family for putting the pictures online?' is a question I have often heard. I am sure many thought it was better to be safe than sorry and decided to keep their collections, even those parts that were well clear of copyright issues, offline. Then, in the European Union (EU) we got the General Data Protection Regulations (GDPR)[3] and the focus and concern shifted slightly towards privacy. Do we have the right to share this information about people? What if they are deceased? Again, unanswered questions, concerns and avoidance of risk.

These issues can be summed up as a matter of 'the right to be forgotten' vs. 'the right to be remembered'. We often see that privileged groups have an easier time being remembered in history, and my worry is that privacy concerns may (sometimes inadvertently) result in keeping certain groups of people from being remembered by history.

Further, copyright law and GDPR were not developed with heritage material in mind, but for different purposes. This is in contrast to heritage laws that often state how people's culture and materials must be protected, recorded and shared for the future. These issues are the subject of Chapter 2.

Chapter 3 introduces the publication of open data, and is aimed at institutions and private individuals who wish to make their datasets available for reuse. It uses the five questions of the Open Heritage Data Model presented in Chapter 1 to evaluate the openness of publications across the GLAM sector through various examples. Heritage data that has been digitised should be put to use. That is the whole purpose of spending millions on this process.

Chapter 4 explores the different aspects of use and reuse of heritage datasets through examples, illustrating how heritage data can be reused for educational purposes, games and guide apps, as well as in do-it-yourself (DIY) and maker culture. The chapter also illustrates how groups of heritage hackers and Wikipedians are collaborating with heritage institutions in order to mediate heritage to new audiences, and how open heritage datasets are used in portals for searching across institutions and collections, as well as various specialised tools.

One of the arguments I often hear that hinders the reuse of heritage data is absence of technical skills and interest. This is my motivation for writing this book and why the chapters that follow include practical coding tutorials that will, it is hoped, inspire readers to begin coding with heritage data. The only prerequisites for this are curiosity and a willingness to experiment. That is my aim, and my own experience with teaching coding and data work in the humanities tells me that this is possible. Even if you, the reader, manage to work through only the first tutorial I would say that you have come a long way towards understanding the rationale for open data in the heritage sector. In this tutorial basic data is reused by pulling data from the API for a poetry database called PoetryDB. This basic code uses PHP: Hypertext Preprocessor (PHP) to visualise the titles of Emily Brontë poems as a simple list. In itself not an amazing visualisation, but, once you have got the hang of pulling data from an API and visualising it on the screen, the tutorials in Chapter 5 move on to visualising images, maps and charts.

In Chapter 6 I introduce the concept of combining different datasets. The chapter is divided into dataset themes, such as combining images of artwork, combining maps of archaeological records or combining newspaper records. The purpose of this chapter is to show how the power of open data enables us to work with not one but several datasets together in combination.

In Chapter 7 I illustrate how open data can be used as research data for further analysis using the coding language Python. The Trove API is used to demonstrate how to perform basic data collection and data cleaning of Australian digitised newspapers. These are then analysed and visualised on a timeline, and this forms the basis of a discussion about the role and validity of OHD for research purposes.

This book presents over 50 different examples (as well as the case examples in Chapter 1) which I have attempted to give a fairly wide geographical spread.[4] Nevertheless, the examples are weighted towards Denmark (my home country) and the USA (see Appendix A); it has also been difficult to get a fair cultural and language spread, language barrier being one reason for this, as I am fluent in only Danish and English. My cultural bias has also made it difficult to search online for open datasets in countries such as South Africa, even though one of the national languages is English: I simply do not know what to search for, and using the search terms I would use in a European or North American context does not yield much. I am hesitant to conclude that there is no OHD in the countries and regions of the world where I have not been able to find it. The fact is, I simply do not know. Further, the examples used throughout the book are not full case studies (unlike those in Chapter 1) of the online publications of heritage institutions. Rather, they are snapshots of certain aspects of these publications at the time of writing this book and are used to illustrate how institutions tackle the different aspects and issues involved in OHD.

I have included interviews from cases and examples that are used throughout the book as well as interviews with key people. All respondents were given a choice of different levels of anonymity. Some wished to be mentioned by name for their contributions, some wished to be acknowledged for their participation and others wished to remain anonymous. These interviews were not conducted as a part of an empirical study, but were used to fill the gaps in my knowledge of this subject. OHD, being a somewhat new field for many, does not yet have a substantial literature.

I have used an autoethnographic approach (Ellis, Adams and Bochner, 2011) throughout the book, using my own observations, experiences and reflections to examine and understand the practices and opinions involved in OHD. This is combined with an applied approach to digital humanities where I have tested a plethora of heritage APIs in order to create the tutorials in Chapters 5–7. Further, my research is based on a culturally critical approach, examining the power dynamics of both heritage and digital technology every step of the way.

Notes

1   An API (Application Programming Interface) is a set of protocols that specify the interaction between data providers and data users over the web. It enables applications to access and interact with live datasets on other servers.

2   See Hamilton and Saunderson (2017) for an overview of open licensing as it relates to heritage.

3   Similar data protection legislation exists around the world.

4   Over 50% of the total are from Europe (with nearly 20% of the total from Denmark and 8% from the UK). About 21% are from North America and the remainder from the rest of the world.

Openness in heritage

From my own perspective, OHD is not so much a technical issue but, rather, about data access being the current frontier in a long line of attempts to open up heritage to a wider group of people. This is the main goal for many GLAM institutions and the people who work in them: to engage a wider population in heritage. This is my goal too, but I do not believe that the heritage community is currently reaching its full potential in this respect. Hence this call to action for OHD.

The introduction examined a number of concepts, among them that of Open Heritage. It is this idea of openness in heritage that is dealt with in this chapter. Before working with the technicalities of OHD it is important that we understand why this is the next step in a long line of both more and less successful attempts to open up heritage.

For me it is not the awe of technology that is the driving force in my long-time interest in this subject. The reason why I work with heritage data is not because today we can make cool, three-dimensional (3D) models and interactive apps. I wish to open up heritage data further, using open data technologies, because it is a vital part of ongoing attempts to open up heritage for all. Many GLAM institutions today have a great focus on being democratic and inclusive. It is time to put those words into action and step up to the latest methods for engagement. It is time to share the raw data, catalogues, images, maps and more that are the basis of these galleries, libraries, archives and museums. Further, it is time for the GLAM sector to band together with the large groups of people working with heritage in their free time. I call them 'heritage amateurs', and with the passion and interest that they pour into their work they are the heart of heritage.

I believe the consequences of not doing this would be a loss of relevance to society and a potential loss of revenue from both public and private funding sources. This would be detrimental to the institutions that we expect to protect our heritage for the future.

This book is aimed at heritage professionals, institutions and communities who also wish to open up their heritage to a wider population, to new interest groups and new communities, but who do not necessarily have the technical ability and know-how to do so. I want to show museums how to share their objects and stories, and to show archives how to share their documents. But first I will discuss how we got to the point of data access so readers can understand the motivation behind this technical work and why it is important heritage work for the future, rather than a subject best left for computer scientists.

This chapter will unfold the idea through a thematic genealogy of heritage organisation and the process of opening up heritage collections to a wider audience. Going back to the beginnings of structured heritage work means looking at heritage amateurs, how they have organised themselves and their collections and how they engage with others. This is followed by a brief description of early institutionalisation and professionalisation, and the chapter ends with three sections about the growing access to heritage: (1) physical access, (2) online access, (3) data access. The themes are presented chronologically, but there is historical and temporal overlap within the themes. I will also add examples and cases throughout. As I attempt to unravel these themes in a way that makes sense across different cultures I am painfully aware that there will be examples and ideas that do not fit with some cultures, infrastructures and jurisdictions. I hope that readers will be able to look past this and understand the broader argumentation behind it.

Heritage amateurs

The word 'amateur' is often misconstrued as meaning a non-expert – so much so that I have often considered simply using a different term. At GLAM seminars in the past I have tried using 'those with a special interest in your subject', and I also have to be very careful to point out that I do not mean museum volunteers, even though there can be some overlap here. I mean amateurs in the historical sense of the word. However, current culture often equates the amateur-professional spectrum to the inept-expert spectrum (Crawford, 2009). This understanding is clear to see in most online thesauri, where a popular suggestion for antonyms of 'expert' is 'amateur'. 'Amateur' comes from the Latin word 'amator' (meaning lover) and literally means someone who is doing something out of love (rather than for compensation) (Oxford Living Dictionaries, 2020). Nevertheless, it is clear that the two meanings of the word have competed with each other for a long time. This is due to the growth of education systems, and thus the growth of the professional sphere. One of the main arguments for following an education is that you become a professional (someone with training) and can charge for your services. This has led to a need to separate the professional from the amateur (someone without training, who is doing it for free and out of interest) on an important parameter, namely expertise. A primary motivation for pursuing an education is the opportunity to become an expert in the chosen area and, ultimately, to make a living by it.

The emergence of new professions was a characteristic trend in 19th-century Western societies; as well as the creation of new types of employment, largely spawned by the needs of a market economy, many of the older professions began to create the elite conditions that we now associate with professional standing. Attempts to limit entry to these avenues of employment through more stringent training and qualifications provided a sense of community and status for those within (Levine, 1986, 6).

Today we are left with these two different definitions of the amateur. One serves the purpose of motivating education and upholding institutional structures, and the second more precisely describes those taking part in activities in a non-professional manner. I will not set out to sway the definition to my way of understanding amateurs, as I do acknowledge that the first definition exists and serves a purpose. However, the second definition is better suited to understanding the amateurs that I will discuss in the following. They are defined by not having a professional training in the heritage activities they undertake.[1] The reasons for this are many. Historically there may not have been any professional training available, or it may not have been available to these people because of their gender, race or socioeconomic status. It may have been available to them, but they may have been self-funded and not in need of employment. They may be professional in another line of work and thus do amateur work in heritage in their free time. Whatever the reason, their attachment to heritage work is out of interest rather than for compensation, and this is how heritage work first started: out of interest, a curiosity towards and perhaps a passion for heritage. So, in order to go back to the beginnings of heritage and heritage collections we need to go back and look at some of the historical heritage amateurs.

More structured heritage work began with amateur communities, dispersed and decentralised and often with a particular focus on local heritage. In modern times it is also amateurs who begin more structured heritage work in subjects and regions where professionals have not yet cast their attention. Their focus may be the heritage of groups of people who are not acknowledged by governments, or areas where governments are not able to fund professional involvement. Here heritage amateurs still play an essential role and can, through their interest in the subject, begin heritage work that, in some cases, is later taken over by heritage professionals when funding becomes more available. In some of these cases we also see heritage professionals and students volunteering alongside heritage amateurs (Sinn, 2017).

Historically these amateur communities were a first step towards opening up heritage to a wider audience. Levine (1986) has studied the minute books of local societies and papers of self-taught archaeologists in order to understand the relationships between amateurs and professionals in heritage fields in 19th-century England. She found that, on the one hand, they generally worked as a community, sharing material and publishing together. On the other hand, their community was small and tight, bound by social and family ties. Many of those involved were male, Anglican and educated at the old universities in some professional sphere that was not necessarily heritage related. This means that while they were generally happy to share and open up heritage among each other, this was not the case in relation to the wider public. This picture of amateur heritage work in England can also be recognised to some extent in the same period in other countries like Denmark, as the folowing Case study of the Mikkelsens illustrates.

Case study 1.1: Christen Mikkelsen and Poul Helweg Mikkelsen

Danish father and son Christen Mikkelsen (1844–1924) and Poul Helweg Mikkelsen (1876–1940) are an example of an amateur interest in heritage with generational continuity and progression. The older Mikkelsen is a good example of what Levine (1986) calls an antiquarian, while the younger Mikkelsen is a very typical amateur archaeologist of his time.

Both were pharmacists, with the son taking over the pharmacy in Odense from his father. The father first found an interest in antiquities at Odense Løveapotek, where, in his younger days he worked under pharmacist Gustav Lotze, who was a member of the first board of the provincial Odense museum. His heritage work was that of a collector. He collected antiquities from the areas where he visited or lived, either by finding them together with his family or by buying them from local farmers. In his will, he left the collection in its entirety to the museum in Odense and asked them to exhibit it as one collection, at a time where most museums were moving towards a chronological framework for exhibits.

The son, Poul Helweg Mikkelsen, on the other hand, was a true amateur archaeologist who gained great experience in conducting archaeological excavations where finds were registered together with context and excavation drawings. The reports are written in a narrative style where decisions and thoughts are noted and later typed up. For example, in interpreting a barrow grave on Farmer Grandt's land in Tirslund, Jutland, he is at first convinced that the occurrence of 18 amber beads means that the deceased was a woman. Together with the group, consisting of his assistant and local interested farmers, he finds a clay pot and a 11.5 cm long granite shaft-hole axe, which resulted in the following comment in the report, translated from Danish:

> It is said that there are no axes in a woman's grave, but are there then amber beads in a man's grave?
>
> This way of questioning the past and our interpretations of it while thoroughly recording all findings together with reflections is very much the cornerstone of archaeological work. It is also something that would not have been possible if Poul Helweg Mikkelsen had just written 'found on field in Tirslund', which was the case with his father's catalogue. Poul Helweg Mikkelsen was very well respected by the few professional archaeologists of the time, and was even involved in training the first professional excavating archaeologist at the provincial museum in Odense.
>
> (Case from [Roued-Cunliffe] Olsen, 2005)

This case shows how early heritage work (albeit a few years later in Denmark than in England) was held together by family and other close ties and relied on reputation among a small group of people. Further, it shows progression in how amateurs conduct heritage work – progression that we can follow from father to son. That is not to say that we do not still have antiquities collectors, as well as both legal and illegal sales of antiquities, today. It merely shows that as the son gained more experience and knowledge in his amateur work, so his work took on a more expert character and his reputation in the heritage field grew as well. However, what did not change was his role as a professional pharmacist and an amateur archaeologist. He gained experience, but not the education and pay that would make him a professional.

Another difference between the father and son is that whereas the father's interactions with heritage were conducted within the closed confines of his own home, with antiquities entering the home but no indication of knowledge leaving a very close group of people with whom he shared his interest (e.g. his wife, family and other collectors), the son is again quite different. He conducts his heritage work out in the countryside, where his reports show the involvement of several other people, from his assistant Harry Hansen to interested locals and perhaps the farmers themselves. In other words, he is opening up heritage to include and engage the interested parts of the local community where he is excavating. Further, he funds the exhibition of his finds, such as the Ladby Ship on Funen. He thus opens up his finds and his knowledge to a wider community.

Organising heritage in institutions

From the last half of the 19th century onwards, heritage institutions in some parts of the world moved away from being established and run by various amateurs, and into a professionalisation phase. Professionals were hired as curators rather than paid caretakers of collections. However, the case study below of Nina Layard demonstrates that this was not necessarily a smooth process. Rather, there was some conflict and a continual overlap between paid and volunteer curators – a system that can still be seen in many institutions today.

Case study 1.2: Nina Frances Layard

Nina Layard (1853–1935) was an English amateur archaeologist who excavated and published Foxhall Road and other Palaeolithic and Anglo-Saxon sites around Ipswich. She came from a wealthy background, being related to people such as Lady Charlotte Schreiber (ceramics collector and museum donor) and Sir Austen Henry Layard (excavator of Nineveh and Nimrud in modern-day Iraq).

Her expertise and social position were not enough, however, to gain her admittance to The Society of Antiquities to deliver a paper on her finds. Even with the support of Sir John Evans, she had to admit defeat and he instead delivered the paper as her sponsor. However, back in Ipswich, where she had donated most of her collection to the museum, her intellectual authority and connections gave her enough clout in comparison to paid curator Frank Woolnough. Her deal with the museum was that she and only she had access to her collection, which was kept under lock and key.

(Case from Hill, 2016, 35–6)

The case illustrates the gender issues involved in professionalisation, which for many years was generally possible only for men. At this point in time volunteering was one of the few options open for women who wished to participate in heritage work (Hill, 2016, 34–5). This uncovers an interesting dilemma in terms of openness in heritage at that time. Institutions and the growing professionalisation of heritage work, with the compensation that followed, opened up the possibility for those from other backgrounds and without self-funding to do heritage work – but in the beginning they were mainly men. On the other side of the coin, in terms of doing heritage work within these new institutions this process closed some of the opportunities for women who had their own sources of funds.

Further, the new institutions meant a formalisation of direct access to heritage materials outside of those items that are visible in the exhibitions. Whereas before access to heritage materials was given through membership of a community of interest or social connections, access to the majority of heritage collections was now primarily given to educated scholars in the field, as well as professional colleagues. Again, the Layard case shows an overlap of two systems, where formalised access was slower to reach provincial institutions. Formalised access still exists today, requiring a person to justify their research credentials and interest in the material in order to be granted access. This can be seen with the Danish Netarchives (netarkivet.dk), a dataset of Danish websites archived from 2005 onwards.

> Netarchive cannot be accessed by the general public. The archive is only
> accessible to researchers who have requested and been granted special
> permission to use the collection for specific research purposes.
>
> (Det Kongelige Bibliotek, 2019)

This is a policy that prioritises educated professionals over interested amateurs and thus would seem to be a closing mechanism rather than a step towards more openness in heritage. However, it can also be seen as a way of opening up heritage to those with an education in heritage – a continually growing group – as opposed to only those with sufficient means and family ties.

This shift towards a more modern museum with professional curation is typically viewed as a way to differentiate the museum from the earlier collections of curiosities meant to amuse and wonder. Some viewed the new way of governing museums as a path away from the 'fossilism or foolish proceedings' of the previously amateur-governed museums (Greenwood, 1888, 4, cited in Bennett, 1995, 2). The newly educated heritage professionals learnt that there was a better way of running a museum and recording history than that which could be seen among those without a heritage education. For a long time, they focused on the proper curation of heritage items, recording and structuring them, and finally presenting them to the public, as we will see in the next section on physical access. This focus has changed in later years toward a greater attention to the visitors or potential visitors of museums.

In my experience there is still a strained relationship between heritage amateurs and professionals across the board. The following Brazilian example illustrates some of this in the relationship between historians (professionals) and family historians (amateurs).

> Professional historians don't usually value Family History. Historiography in
> Brazil is very discipline oriented. Oriented towards the historical discipline as a
> serious Social Science. Many of the 1960s and 1970s historical works that helped
> to build this disciplinary conscience and sense of social duty among our
> historians were not concerned (at all) with family but the working class, social
> economy and politics. Family history probably would be considered as an
> 'amateurish' endeavour with no real 'social interest'. Besides, to focus on a
> 'family' (like the historian's family) was considered bias and not scientific. It was
> ideologically related with conservative thinking, or associated with too much of a
> 'petite-bourgeoisie' thing, or a 'pre-modern' (anachronistic) value, a 'petite

histoire' or 'ego history' at best, not much value as scientific research. Historians were (some still are) very concerned with the big socially relevant questions and problems they thought kept Brazil from its full development and modernization. The power and influence of some families' private interest over the public sphere (politics, public administration, economy and so on) was huge and, therefore, a problem.

(A. de L. Freixo, personal communication, 2019)

I remember how exasperated I would become as an archaeology student on excavations if members of the public suggested that I was working as an archaeologist merely out of a personal interest. I was a professional, or at least I was going to be a professional archaeologist – and I wanted a proper pay for my work, recognition that my work was valued by the wider public (something that I did not take for granted). What I did not understand at the time, but have later come to realise, was that my field would never be truly valued if I and my fellow heritage colleagues insisted on keeping heritage amateurs and their passion for heritage at arm's length.

I believe that the need to keep this distinction between heritage professionals and amateurs in the foundation of our heritage institutions is to some extent due to a feeling of insecurity among professionals. In today's political climate, with ongoing cuts to heritage and culture budgets (Sanderhoff, 2017, 108), it would be natural to fear for your job in the sector and perhaps be wary of anyone who might want to do it for free.

However, when I look at the leisure field of sport (which I will admit is not my research subject) it seems to me that having many players on an amateur level brings attention, volunteers and further funding to professional players and sport as a whole. Further, it means that more children are able to take an interest in sport because it is a popular and available pastime in their local communities. All in all, I think that a good relationship between amateurs and professionals brings value to the institutions, professionals and the field as a whole. It becomes more relevant to society and gets better funding. I wonder if, and how, this can be further emulated in the heritage sector.

Physical access

Ruge et al. have identified five issues that help to explain why Australian historical societies are reluctant to share material online (Ruge et al., 2017, 82; see Chapter 2 for a further review of the issues in full).

Of these, the belief that physical access meets most needs is particularly interesting, as physical access to heritage in institutions was such a great step in the genealogy of openness in heritage. Because it is unclear to what extent they were open to the public, it is difficult to determine which museum is the oldest public museum. Some of the currently known oldest heritage collections open to the public were established in Europe from the 15th to 17th centuries. The fact that anyone who was in the proximity and could afford the entry price was permitted access to view collections on display was revolutionary, but this did not happen from day one. For example, the Royal Armouries in the Tower of London were first open to a more privileged group of visitors during the 15th and 16th century and became open to a paying public from 1660 (Royal Armouries, 2019). Prior to this public access, all heritage material was accessible to view only if one was a part of or had ties to the small group of heritage amateurs. That being said, a large amount of heritage material is still unavailable to the wider public even today, because it is stored out of sight and not published.

Nevertheless, from this perspective physical access to a heritage collection from 10:00 am until 5:00 pm, Tuesday till Sunday[2] can be seen as another step towards further openness. The general population has access to come and see the material. It is no longer hidden (apart from all the items in storage). In order to move on with open data in a meaningful way we must first acknowledge that for many people physical openness is not only enough but also a huge step forward from a system where only select scholars are allowed access. The only access or engagement that the working-class previously had to heritage (apart from their own living heritage) was when they worked as paid or volunteer labour on excavations led and funded by amateur archaeologists, as in the cases of Nina Layard or Poul Helweg Mikkelsen, or when they found heritage material and sold it on to antiquities collectors like Christen Mikkelsen.

Physical access to heritage material for anyone (who can pay for access) is an important part of the genealogy of open heritage. But physical access alone is not enough in a time where many people find themselves going online to seek information and entertainment, using digital methods to create and share their knowledge and creativity. The lack of online access to heritage material becomes a stumbling block that stunts creative expression and innovative development, as well as wider access for those who do not have the means to travel to get physical access.

Further, there are also conservation issues with physical access, in that many heritage items are fragile and would not survive everyone having access to handle them. Therefore, digitising them gives more people an opportunity to 'handle' at least a version of them.

Historical societies in Australia are not alone in thinking that physical access to their heritage material and data is more than enough. I believe the reason for this to be a difficulty in imagining that there is actually someone sitting across the country, let alone across the world, who might also have an interest in their heritage material. For these people physical access is no access at all. Even if all their material is nicely documented in a database, this still implies physical access if a person is required to visit the institution to use the database or see the collection.

Another hindrance in making heritage material openly accessible is the erroneous belief that the heritage it represents is not universally interesting. It might not be of international, national or even regional importance and as such may not be considered serious heritage (Howard, 2003, 4); but if family historians have taught us one thing it is that even the most obscure, local heritage is of interest to someone else, and that someone may very well live on the other side of the world. When we consider the historical migration of people and how this can play a role in a family's history, it actually seems more likely that they *will* live on the other side of the world than in the neighbouring town. For example, a Danish person such as me may want to know how life was for their ancestors moving to Chicago in the USA in the 1880s. Another example could be an American with Indian heritage wanting to understand how life was for their family before they left for the USA. There are many examples across the world – I have several in my own family, as do most family historians I have ever met.

However, it is very difficult to get access to material and information on heritage from a distance. Even if the information exists, it may be accessible only locally in a physical or even digital format. Thus it is not only inaccessible, but also undiscoverable, as was the case with the No Gun Ri material (Case study 1.3). We will never even know that it is there, let alone how to access it.

Case study 1.3: No Gun Ri Digital Archive

The No Gun Ri Massacre refers to the mass killing of refugees in 1950 in South Korea by US military troops. It was only half a century later, thanks to an Associated Press report (Sang-Hun, Hanley and Mendoz, 1999), that the story became internationally known. In 2009 the No Gun Ri Peace Park and Museum was established, largely based on the materials and work of the Chung family, survivors and historians of the massacre.

The No Gun Ri Digital Archive project (nogunri.rit.albany.edu) was initiated by Donghee Sinn in 2012 and has since received several small grants in order to digitise and publish archival material and oral stories about the massacre. However, no one in the digital project is directly associated with the No Gun Ri Museum or any survivors, meaning that their physical access to any material is limited by the direct access given by the museum. One of the main challenges faced by the digital archival project was that project members had to devote time to travel to the museum in order to visit and digitise the collection, often in a volunteer capacity (Sinn, 2017). The main benefit of the digital archive over the physical one is that it is accessible via a simple web search and does not require prior knowledge about archives in general or about the No Gun Ri archive specifically (D. Sinn, personal communication, 2019).

Online access

When we talk about online access this relates closely to digital or virtual access. In the case of heritage items, digital access often means access to the digitised version of the items – in other words, a copy. Unlike items that are born digital (created computationally, and having a whole range of other issues when it comes to archiving for the future), digitised representations of analogue items are translations of the item, and not the items themselves (Terras, 2015a).

It is not the real thing and it cannot replace the feeling, sound, smell or experience of the real thing. I recently watched a video shared on social media by the Natural History Museum, London in which British broadcaster and natural historian Sir David Attenborough meets himself in virtual reality in the Sky Virtual Reality app 'Hold the World' (Natural History Museum, London, 2018). In this environment a dinosaur flies at him, making him raise his arms ready to defend himself – altogether an amazing experience, I'm sure, but not one that can substitute for 50 years of travelling the Earth and seeing nature from an extremely privileged vantage point. However, we must remember two things: first, that there are very few people as privileged as Attenborough who are able to have these experiences in real life and most rely on his many films to replicate this. Second, even Attenborough will never experience a dinosaur in real life. While the experience of smell, touch and feel is important and no digital version can replicate this, digital and online access can do so much more.

First and foremost, it can give you access to many things that you would never be able to experience in real life, such as dinosaurs, life in an Iron Age village and heritage items that are outside your personal reach due to travel or monetary restrictions. Second, online access can make you aware of heritage that you might be able to visit only once you know that it exists.

Digital content can be browsed easily and can be searched, indexed or collated instantly. Most importantly, it can be linked to a whole 'web' of other content, either locally or globally, via the internet (Hughes, 2004).

Online access to heritage material has had an immense impact on the way special-interest communities do heritage work. Nowhere is this clearer than in family history, one of the most common historical activities in the world (De Groot, 2009, 73). Every day more and more heritage material becomes available online that can be accessed and used in family research, whether you are sitting at the archive or in a public library on the other side of the world (Jurczyk-Romanowska and Tufekčić, 2018). The world's largest family history site, Ancestry.com, currently has three million paying subscribers, and together, Ancestry members from 80 different countries of origin have created 100 million family trees.[3] Family historians are thus the largest heritage interest group and the one most active on the web. Here they use online heritage material such as parish records and population censuses, photographs, maps, public records and private papers as well as information about places, people, occupations and more to gain insights into their own heritage. Further, they use the internet to engage in mass-transcription projects, as we see in the case of the Lancashire Online Parish Clerks project (Case study 1.4). In addition to their significant transcription and collection efforts, many are willing to learn new technologies in order to improve or extend the capabilities of their projects (Ridge, 2017, 63).

While heritage professionals may not directly see the need to engage with family history, they must be aware that 'almost every heritage item has another set of personal meanings to someone, and that every visitor to official, managed heritage arrives with a personal baggage containing a heritage which they regard as much more important' (Howard, 2003, 4).

Case study 1.4: Online Parish Clerks in Lancashire

Lancashire Online Parish Clerks is one of several UK Online Parish Clerks projects with a focus on freely publishing online the historical parish records, in this case from the county of Lancashire (lan-opc.org.uk). The project began in 2003, inspired by other Online Parish Clerks projects in the UK. The founder, Paul Dixon, invited other contributors to a regional genealogy forum and together they built the current website, which went live in February 2004. One of the great tasks in the beginning was to define a format in which to store the data they were collecting, as well as methods for retrieving the data through searching and browsing. Everything in the project has been developed by a group of heritage amateurs.

Nevertheless, the group had a strong motivation to make Lancashire heritage records available online. When asked, members say that the fact that the project is non-commercial and that they get good feedback from grateful genealogy researchers is also motivation that enables them to keep working on the project. This is understandable, as the project is very successful, with an estimated 100 active transcribers, perhaps one third of them from outside the UK. The site has approximately 8000 distinct users a week and receives around 100,000 hits a day.

While the current website, built in HTML with no content management system or database behind it, publishes the dataset free for anyone to use, the project team is currently not interested in making the dataset available through, for example, an API. There are several reasons for this. One is that they are concerned about making the dataset available so that anyone can use it for commercial purposes. Another is that they are unsure whether the permissions they have to publish the data would cover this. (Lancashire Online Parish Clerks, personal communication, 2019)

GLAM institutions make heritage material available online for anyone to search and browse. This gives family historians and many others a great opportunity to find information. However, there are still obstacles in terms of reusing the material. Family historians are a good example of this, as they typically structure the information they find about their family into digital and/or online family trees with their own set of formats. Just like professional historians, experienced family historians know to record the source of this information as a vital aspect of historical research. However, while many platforms have emerged over the years enabling the discovery of historical source material, I have yet to see a platform that enables downloads, links or exporting options into one of these family history systems. The platforms we usually see are full of valuable information, but they are typically difficult to navigate and often lack permanent linking options. In other words, while online access has meant a great deal for openness towards new communities that otherwise would not realistically have had physical access to the material, it rarely makes collections available for reuse on other platforms or in other systems.

Further, many countries have copyright laws that allow educational institutions, libraries and visually impaired people to have more copyright privileges and exemptions than the rest of the population (Cornish, 2015, 18). But as soon as the conversation turns to openness and opening up to those outside these communities, on the World Wide Web, there are difficulties. Sharing datasets with colleagues who contact you directly means that you can check up on them and keep an eye on what they are doing with the material; but what happens when anyone can access and use your data because it's freely and technically available on the internet? This is something that the heritage sector is still struggling with, and copyright has in many ways come to embody this discussion (see Chapter 2).

Outside the heritage sector, in the music industry, the film industry and many other creative industries, they have the same struggle, and copyright is very big business indeed. It seems that much of our copyright law and practice today is still aimed at these areas, and this is perhaps why it is very difficult to understand copyright in the context of heritage data. However, one important thing to remember about copyright is the motivation for the law. Copyright should act as a motivation to create, because you know that you are the owner of your creative work and thus have certain rights over it (Cornish, 2015).

Therefore, online access is not enough for the purposes of creativity. While the ability to see and read about heritage material online, and perhaps to copy and paste or download for personal use, has meant a great deal to many, it is still not enough to encourage innovation and creativity. It has provided many people who have been physically or socially distanced from the material with the means and opportunity to study and be inspired by it, but it has not given them the ability to use and reuse the material for new purposes. This is where the idea of OHD comes in.

Data access

The Open Knowledge Foundation states: 'Open means anyone can freely access, use, modify and share for any purpose (subject, at most, to requirements that preserve provenance and openness)' (Open Knowledge International, 2019a). Here the focus is very much on enabling reuse of knowledge in a data format, with special emphasis on knowledge being available and openly licensed. However, for clarity, this definition of open data does not encourage the sharing of sensitive and/or personal data of living people (Open Knowledge International, 2019b).

Linked Open Data (LOD), the brainchild of Tim Berners-Lee and W3C (the World Wide Web Consortium), emulates the idea behind open knowledge through the 5-star LOD scheme. The fifth star is given only to datasets that provide links to other people's data and use URIs (Uniform Resource Identifiers) to identify data elements in line with ideas of the Semantic Web[4] (Berners-Lee, 2009).

The OpenGLAM initiative has worked on a set of principles that are championed by OpenGLAM institutions. The first principle is to 'release digital information about the artefacts (metadata) into the public domain using an appropriate legal tool such as the Creative Commons Zero Waiver' (OpenGLAM, 2019). In other words, to ensure the discoverability of material, whether this be artefacts, images, maps, videos, lists and so forth. In heritage, metadata is important, and making metadata available is the first step towards ensuring that heritage material is shared not just through personal connections.

The second principle is to 'Keep digital representations of works for which copyright has expired (public domain) in the public domain by not adding new rights to them' (OpenGLAM, 2019). This can be seen as a direct criticism of heritage institutions that scour copyright law for loopholes to retain the copyright on material they are responsible for digitising. Interpretations of copyright law in some countries state that if the digitisation of analogue material constitutes a creative process by a human being (e.g. adjusting light, etc.) and is not just an automated machine process (e.g. using a scanner), then the human or the workplace has copyright of the digitised version (Cornish, 2015). The ethics of this approach can be discussed, particularly if the work is done through public funding, by a public institution or through volunteer work (Petri, 2014).

The third principle states: 'When publishing data make an explicit and robust statement of your wishes and expectations with respect to reuse and repurposing of the descriptions, the whole data collection and subsets of the collection' (OpenGLAM, 2019). What this means is that the institution making data available online needs to make sure that they are knowledgeable about copyright first and foremost, and to be very clear about how material can be reused or not. Reuse is a big part of the internet, and has been from the beginning. Publishing online means that everyone can technically reuse the material, whether they are allowed to or not. However, with more and more heritage material available online for reuse, I fear there is an even bigger risk that material published without open licensing will lie unused and forgotten. Another thing to be aware of is the issue of commercial use, as it is now generally accepted that commercial use can be anything from posting on a blog that earns advertising revenue to use by large, multibillion-dollar industries. This has given birth to the Free Culture Movement, with a focus on availability for reuse, which also champions reuse for commercial purposes (Freedom Defined, 2015).

The fourth principle reads: 'When publishing data use open file formats which are machine-readable' (OpenGLAM, 2019). This means not using proprietary formats that can be accessed only by certain computer programs that require licences. Open machine-readable formats include many different formats depending on the nature of the material and its use. In essence, a comma-separated values (CSV) file is open and machine readable, but a web service with JavaScript Object Notation (JSON) data format would be even more so. Data documentation is also an important thing to remember here. Without good documentation your well-intended open data is just as unlikely to be used as the many boxes stacked in your remote storage.

The fifth and last principle states: 'Opportunities to engage audiences in novel ways on the web should be pursued' (OpenGLAM, 2019). In essence, this requires funding and an overall strategy for open data. This is also one of the most important parts of open data, and where it most often fails. We put data on the web, we say 'come and use it', but we rarely engage actively with the people who would potentially want to use it. This is not only about going to hackathons and encouraging programmers to develop stuff with your datasets. This is also about thinking outside the box and considering who could benefit from your data. School children and teachers, perhaps;

well, then you need to get in contact with them to see how they could use it. Students, perhaps; then reach out to relevant departments or, even better, lecturers teaching relevant subjects. Amateurs; reach out to the groups that are organised already. Ask for membership of existing Facebook groups on local history or amateur archaeology; the likelihood of these groups approaching you is very small if you are just starting out with open data. However, this is something that requires resources and dedicated staff in order to facilitate, and should never be a small-add on to the main development work.

Table 1.1 summarises these three definitions and principles for open data. Open Knowledge focuses on reuse in general terms, LOD focuses on connecting data and OpenGLAM focuses on issues particular to GLAM institutions. I have combined these into five questions into the OHD Model, which can be used to evaluate how open a particular heritage dataset is.

Table 1.1 *Definitions and principles of openness for the Open Knowledge Foundation, LOD and OpenGLAM*

Open Knowledge	LOD	OpenGLAM
Open licence or status	Online with open licence	Release metadata on artefacts
Access	Machine-readable structured data	No new digital copyright to works in public domain
Machine readability	Non-proprietary format	Be clear about reuse of published data
Open format	Open standards from W3C (RDF [Resource Description Framework] and SPARQL)	Use machine-readable open file formats
	Linked to other people's data	Engage with the public about the open content

1 Is the material published online, with metadata so that it can be searched and filtered?
2 Is the material published with an open licence or in the public domain, and is this clearly communicated in conjunction with the material?
3 Does the institution actively encourage reuse of the material and provide support for anyone who wishes to reuse it, free of charge?
4 Is the material available in an open, machine-readable format that anyone can export/download?
5 Is the material available through a well-described web service or API that anyone has access to?

Although it is clear that a positive answer to question 1 constitutes much less openness than a positive answer to question 5, it is not the intention to develop a five-star rating system as with LOD (Berners-Lee, 2009). Instead, these five questions can be used to understand rather than evaluate the degree to which GLAM institutions are opening up their heritage data. These questions will be used in Chapter 3 to discuss how open the publication of heritage datasets is, through examples that focus on images as well as structured and geographical data.

The least degree of openness which answers positive on the first question of the OHD Model is found in online publications of heritage material with metadata that can be browsed and searched. An example of this is the Arab Image Foundation's website (arabimagefoundation.com). The Arab Image Foundation (AIF) is a Beirut (Lebanon) based non-profit archive of Middle Eastern photography. The director of the AIF, Marc Mourakech, intends the website to engage people in a participatory process of image collection and documentation. The AIF recognises the importance both of opening up heritage towards the general public and of engaging amateurs and private collectors, 'against a backdrop of growing concern over the condition of regional state archives amid political upheaval' (Cornwell, 2019). On the Foundation's website, images in the dataset are available with metadata, such as photographer, date, photographic process (e.g. gelatine silver negative on glass), dimensions, deterioration and physical markings (e.g. discoloration, mirroring, oxidation, peeling, water damage) and original item status.

The second question asks whether the material published online is free of copyright restrictions and whether this is communicated for each item. The National Gallery of Denmark (SMK; smk.dk) have made a commitment to opening up their collection and have so far published 79,004 items with metadata in an online portal where they can be searched and filtered by, for example, artist, technique and date – as well as an open licence. Figure 1.1 on the next page shows how each artwork is displayed along with the licence by each image. Not every item in this database has an open licence or is in the public domain, but for those that have, it is clearly communicated through the CC0 licence. The licence by the image functions as a link to the Creative Commons website page, which describes each licence in detail (see Chapter 2 for more on open licensing).

The third question focuses on actively encouraged reuse of the material published, as well as some support towards this. The Dutch Rijksmuseum (Museum of the Netherlands; rijksmuseum.nl) have made their collections available as open data through the Rijksstudio application. Here you can search the collection and create a Rijksstudio account that enables you to make your own art collections (see more in Chapter 3). In the Rijksstudio you can also order prints or download the image for any other use if it is in the public domain (Figure 1.2). In other words, they encourage reuse, and also actively facilitate it.

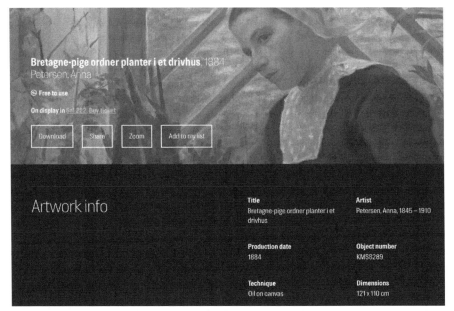

Figure 1.1 *Screenshot of the SMK collection (National Gallery of Denmark, smk.dk). The image is an oil painting, Breton Girl Looking After Plants in the Hothouse, by Anna Petersen (1884), CC0*

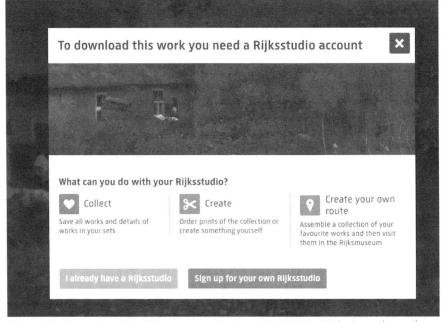

Figure 1.2 *Screenshot of the Rijksmuseum collection (rijksmuseum.nl). The image is an oil painting The Vegetable Garden, by Anton Mauve (c. 1885–8), public domain*

The fourth question looks at whether the material is available for downloading in an open machine-readable format. As with the fourth OpenGLAM principle, this refers to a digital format that is non-proprietary and can be opened in a variety of software. This is exemplified by the Portable Antiquities Scheme (PAS) run by the British Museum and Amgueddfa Cymru/National Museum Wales in the UK (finds.org.uk). The goal of PAS is to encourage the recording of archaeological objects found by members of the public in England and Wales. Without this project, vast amounts of archaeological objects – for example, those found through metal detecting – would go unrecorded. The scheme and database have been running since 1999 and the latter currently consists of nearly 1.5 million objects. Both search results and single records can be downloaded in various formats such as XML, JSON and PDF (Portable Document Format), which can be opened in spreadsheets and software for geographical and other analysis.

The fifth question refers to the highest degree of openness in online publishing of heritage material, namely publication through a well-described web service or API.[5] APIs allow external applications to interact with a dataset through HTTP (HyperText Transfer Protocol) methods such as GET, PUT or DELETE. In the case of open data, we will primarily be using the GET method to retrieve search results from various resources. As an example, we might want to search the dataset from Trove (trove.nla.gov.au), the National Library of Australia, for any records related to the term 'garden' in their newspaper collection. We do this by using an HTTP request through the following URL:

```
https://api.trove.nla.gov.au/v2/result?q=garden&zone=newspaper&encoding=json
```

1 'https://api.trove.nla.gov.au/v2' specifies the dataset we are calling, in this case Trove's dataset;
2 'results' will retrieve a list of results from the dataset;
3 'q=gardening' is the query for the data we want to retrieve – in this case related to the term 'garden';
4 'zone=newspaper' because we want to search newspapers in Trove. The material in Trove is divided into ten zones with different content in each zone (e.g. newspapers, maps, books, photographs, etc.);
5 'encoding=json' because we want to get the result in a JSON format. By default Trove returns data in an XML format.

Part of the returned dataset can be viewed in Figure 1.3 on the next page and is human readable for those who are familiar with JSON code. But, most importantly, the data is machine readable, 'enabling you to create new applications, tools and interface', as the Trove website puts it (Trove, 2019a).

Trove API Console

Explore the workings of the Trove API

https://api.trove.nla.gov.au/v2/result?q=gardening&zone=newspaper&encoding=json   [Go!]   Clear

Enter an API query to view the results (no key required), or start with one of the examples below.

```
{
    "response": {
        "query": "gardening",
        "zone": [
            {
                "name": "newspaper",
                "records": {
                    "s": "*",
                    "n": "20",
                    "total": "9607403",
                    "next": "/result?q=gardening&encoding=json&zone=newspaper&s=AoIIRW16vyg30DQ4MDI4Mg%3D%3D",
                    "nextStart": "AoIIRW16vyg30DQ4MDI4Mg==",
                    "article": [
                        {
                            "id": "183374220",
                            "url": "/newspaper/183374220",
                            "heading": "GARDENING.",
                            "category": "Article",
                            "title": {
                                "id": "463",
                                "value": "The Burrowa News (NSW : 1874 - 1951)"
                            },
                            "date": "1876-08-12",
                            "page": 4,
                            "pageSequence": 4,
                            "relevance": {
                                "score": "3799.6716",
                                "value": "very relevant"
                            },
                            "snippet": "THE following is an extract from a paper read at the last monthly meeting of the New South Wales Hort
                            icultural Society by Mr. John Gelding:— Members of such societies as these can impart",
```

Figure 1.3 *Screenshot of the Trove API Console (troveconsole.herokuapp.com) by Tim Sherratt showing results in JSON format of a request for newspaper articles about 'gardening'*

The machine-readable data from PAS and the machine-readable data from Trove can seem very similar, using the same formats, like JSON and XML. The big difference lies in the reuse options for these datasets. For PAS you must first find the data you need in the online database and then download it. Once it is downloaded the dataset becomes a static representation of the data at the time of downloading. If you want to update your dataset, you must search the PAS database again and export a new dataset. This is fine if you are doing a scientific analysis of the data, where you do not want your results to change every day but instead need a stable snapshot of the data. However, if you want to build an application, tool or interface based on the dataset it becomes important that you have a way of continually accessing the most current version of the dataset through a URL (Uniform Resource Locator) that can be inserted into your code (as we shall see in the examples in Chapter 5). It is also important that the data provider encourages this type of use by providing stable URLs so that the application you have built does not fail all of a sudden because the data it uses is no longer available.

Another reason why downloadable datasets are not really a viable option for developing innovative applications is explained by heritage developer Monique Szpak:

There is also a great deal of cultural open data that is not available via an API but as downloadable datasets – given that my projects tend to be free to use I cannot really afford to host data myself.

(M. Szpak, personal communication, 2019)

In other words, because of funding constraints, for her private side-projects, such as the Culture Collage (see Chapter 4), Szpak can use only data available through APIs. This is also the case for many others who use OHD. Rarely do they have the option of downloading and hosting datasets for projects that they are working on in their free time.

Thus, data access, just like physical and online access, can come in many shapes, from datasets that are online to search and filter, to datasets that are available through an API in a live version for applications, research and interesting new tools. The OHD Model provides a framework for considering how open a dataset can and should be made. This is dependent on the aims of the heritage institution. While this can form part of a formal strategy, it can also happen in a more experimental manner, as is illustrated in the case of Aagaard's Photos (Case study 1.5).

Case study 1.5: Aagaard's Photos

Kolding City Archives (stadsarkiv.kolding.dk) in Denmark made headlines in 2015 when a dataset they had published with photographs taken by Dines Christian Jochum Pontoppidan Aagaard between 1857 and 1880 gained popularity on Facebook. Aagaard had used the early technique of collodion negatives to take portraits of local citizens in the region. The photographs have name tags, and the archive decided to reach out to Danish family history Facebook groups and a local nostalgia Facebook group to ask for help with identifying the people in the portraits. All portraits and biographical information became immediately available online as open datasets for anyone to use through easily accessible sites such as Flickr.com, Google Spreadsheets and Google Maps. This, in itself, is a great motivation for family historians to contribute to a crowdsourcing project as they can directly benefit from the dataset they have helped to create: they can use it to find their own ancestors.

The city archive has benefited in many ways from making this material available as open data. The exposure they gained in the press came as the result of a group of heritage amateurs (interested in family and local history) using and discussing the portraits in their respective Facebook groups. To date, because of this openness the project has resulted in collaborations and partnerships with artists, students, scholars, hackers and other institutions and has given the archive a solid network of heritage amateurs to work with. In the words of city archivist Lene Wul, 'It is difficult to say exactly how, but the openness that began with the Aagaard project has helped to

> establish us as a frontrunner within the local community and the larger heritage sector. It has taught me the importance of letting go of control and making heritage amateurs feel welcome by encouraging them to take ownership over heritage and contribute with their knowledge and time.' (Roued-Cunliffe, 2018; L. Wul, personal communication, 2019)

With the Aagaard's Photos case we see a dataset that became available as open data, with open licensing, using existing platforms like Flickr and Google. There was no expensive, custom-built website and the whole project took off within a couple of months. It was perhaps more a question of luck, rather than of determination, but the project found a group of users among heritage amateurs at a very early stage for whom the dataset was immensely useful. Through this, the archive has gained a great deal, especially in terms of reputation, both locally and nationally. Because of this, the archive is more relevant in the local community and it therefore becomes easier to find new partnerships and funding for projects. All of this would not have been possible if the archive had not been willing to experiment with the ideas of open data.

Summary

This chapter has:

1   explored a journey from the beginnings of structured heritage work, through early institutionalisation and professionalisation, to a thematically chronological description of the phases of increasing access to heritage;
2   introduced the current final step of access to open data through datasets that are online, freely accessible, structured, openly licensed and can be accessed in such a way that they can be reused in new ways for visualisation, research, art, family history, education and much more;
3   explored the degree of open data in the heritage sector through the OHD Model, with five questions covering: (1) online publication with metadata, (2) open licensing, (3) encouraging reuse, (4) machine readable data, (5) APIs.

Notes

1   For a more in-depth discussion of the differences between amateurs and professionals see Stebbins (1979)

2 Monday is traditionally a day when many museums are closed, because they are open during the weekend.

3 As of 22 October 2019 (Ancestry, 2019)

4 The Semantic Web is a World Wide Web Consortium (W3C) vision of a web of linked data (e.g. dates, geography, people, books and much more) (W3C, 2015).

5 A web service and an API are not entirely the same thing but for the purpose of data sharing between heritage institutions they have been used interchangeably, with APIs currently being the preferred term.

## 2

Sharing legally

Open GLAM and data sharing must of course be legal. However, most laws are rarely made with heritage in mind. These laws can be difficult to understand, especially how they apply to our heritage material. This lays the ground for uncertainty and can result in a lack of innovation, due to the fear of getting it wrong. In my opinion, the potential long-term consequences of not opening up heritage can be worse than the risk of making a legal mistake. We need knowledge in order to make a suitable risk analysis. We need knowledge in order to be brave and make bold choices. We need knowledge in order to follow Michael Edson's advice to the SMK: 'Think Big. Start Small. Move Fast' (Sanderhoff, 2017).[1]

There are many reasons given for why heritage institutions and community groups are wary of sharing their collections online.

Based on a study of social media alongside digital image collections by Australian cultural institutions and community archives, researchers found that a lack of digitisation and social media usage could be explained by the following issues:

- questions of ownership (in many cases photographs have been donated, with many sourced from personal family albums or professional studios);
- the belief that physical access to the collections meets most needs;
- concerns regarding the unauthorised reuse of images;
- concerns over losing revenue streams (that is, the ability to sell digital copies of images);
- concerns regarding infringement of copyright or privacy regulations infringement. (Ruge et al., 2017, 82)

Further, the Digital Dilemmas project, with the aim of developing an online catalogue for the Australian Lesbian and Gay Archives (alga.org.au), found issues in regard to ethics and data privacy.

Apart from the belief that physical access meets most needs (covered in Chapter 1) all the other issues have their roots in legal text.

Some larger institutions around the world have access to legal advisors with a good grasp of what copyright and data protection law means for them, and some have perhaps been able to influence these laws. However, it is not my impression that all the laws in question have been developed with the heritage community in mind, let alone in collaboration with heritage communities. Nevertheless, they are usually laws which we in the heritage community have to understand and deal with. This often results in a great deal of frustration and uncertainty in the community at large, and I fear that this uncertainty often results in stagnation when it comes to opening up heritage collections. Even when new heritage portals are published, like the AIF website, launched in 2019 (see Chapter 1), the images are available only to browse and look at. Although the AIF write that they encourage the use of the images for 'artistic, educational and scholarly purposes' (Arab Image Foundation, 2019), the uses have to be non-commercial and non-derivative, and this policy in reality means that the images have very little usefulness for artists, educators, scholars or anyone else. I will discuss this further under free culture licensing.

This is the fear of doing the wrong thing; the fear of doing something illegal that can bring the organisers or their institution or community into jeopardy with the law; the fear of doing something unethical that can give rise to serious controversy in the news or on social media.

The heritage sector needs innovation and experimentation, and this is difficult to sustain in an environment of fear. Institutions may think that they are playing it safe by keeping digitised material offline, or publishing online in such a way that it can only be browsed, but not reused. But it may turn out that a heritage institution 'that restricts public access more than necessary, however carefully explained, would soon find itself starved of tax-payers' funds' (Howard, 2003, 224). This argument was first put forward by Howard in relation to nature conservation in 2003, but I think it is just as relevant to quote in this case.

Further, we could question the ethics of not making heritage material that has been stored and digitised through public funding and/or volunteer work openly accessible if at all possible (Petri, 2014).

Working with digital data and online heritage has changed in recent years. Some of us who have worked with it for a while have had a perhaps naive idea of all the amazing things this new, online world could bring to our common heritage.

Fifteen years ago, Lorna Hughes cited the DigiCULT view that:

Digitisation contributes to the conservation and preservation of heritage and scientific resources; it creates new educational opportunities; it can be used to encourage tourism; and it provides ways of improving access by the citizens to their patrimony.

(DigiCULT, 2003)

According to Hughes, we had come a long way from the 'hollow pronouncements and promises' of ten or fifteen years earlier, in which it was suggested that digital technology 'would save millions of hours of teaching time and increase academic productivity', as well as replace instructors and face-to-face classes with a CD-ROM of a term's coursework (Hughes, 2004, 7).

Looking back over the period since 1990 it is clear to me that digital technology has not been able to replace human tasks, but may instead have added to them. Further, the digitisation of heritage collections over the years has not had the impact that is suggested in the DigiCULT view. That is not to say that digitisation cannot have an impact at all but, rather, that it cannot stand alone. Digitisation without open access and open data impacts on very few.

In this chapter I will not be giving legal advice. It is up to the reader to examine and understand which laws are relevant for their country and type of material. I will, however, give an overview of which types of laws and policies are important to understand, as well as discussing the political and ethical issues around them. Laws are not static; they are a part of our culture and change according to political directions in our society. Therefore, this chapter should be seen as an exploration of which laws are in play now with relation to OHD, as well as a critical examination of these policies. At the end of each section I will add a set of questions that can be used to learn more about these laws in your country or region.

Heritage laws

The UNESCO 1972 World Heritage Convention is ratified by most countries in the world.[2] It aims to link together the preservation of both natural heritage and cultural heritage in one document. The motivation for the Convention is the continual threat to world heritage from decay over time, on the one hand, and the dangers of changing social and economic conditions, such as construction work, conflict and more, on the other hand. The original Convention considers cultural heritage as monuments, buildings and sites:

monuments: architectural works, works of monumental sculpture and painting, elements or structures of an archaeological nature, inscriptions, cave dwellings

and combinations of features, which are of outstanding universal value from the point of view of history, art or science;
groups of buildings: groups of separate or connected buildings which, because of their architecture, their homogeneity or their place in the landscape, are of outstanding universal value from the point of view of history, art or science;
sites: works of man or the combined works of nature and man, and areas including archaeological sites which are of outstanding universal value from the historical, aesthetic, ethnological or anthropological point of view.

(UNESCO, 1972, Article 1)

In addition to this list of UNESCO protected heritage there is the 2003 Convention[3] for the Safeguarding of the Intangible Cultural Heritage, which aims to 'safeguard a specific form of (intangible) heritage: practices, representations, expressions, knowledge and skills that communities recognise as their cultural heritage' (UNESCO ICH, 2019). These could be:

- oral traditions and expressions, including language as a vehicle of the intangible cultural heritage;
- performing arts;
- social practices, rituals and festive events;
- knowledge and practices concerning nature and the universe;
- traditional craftsmanship. (UNESCO, 2003)

Both convention texts mention some sort of sharing of these different types and representations of heritage around the world. The 1972 Convention states that each state party shall endeavour 'to take the appropriate legal, scientific, technical, administrative and financial measures necessary for the identification, protection, conservation, presentation and rehabilitation of this heritage' (UNESCO, 1972, 72, Article 5.4).

The 2003 Convention states that: '"Safeguarding" means measures aimed at ensuring the viability of the intangible cultural heritage, including the identification, documentation, research, preservation, protection, promotion, enhancement, transmission, particularly through formal and non-formal education, as well as the revitalization of the various aspects of such heritage' (UNESCO, 2003, Article 2.3). The last part of this statement – that is, the mandate not only to protect and document but also to present and transmit the heritage that each state is responsible for, and to do this through both formal and non-formal education – is of particular interest for this book.

While the convention texts do not mention data or digitisation as such, the operational directives of the 2003 Convention do. The latest directive, from 2018, states that:

> Research institutes, centres of expertise, museums, archives, libraries,
> documentation centres and similar entities play an important role in collecting,
> documenting, archiving and conserving data on intangible cultural heritage, as
> well as in providing information and raising awareness about its importance [...]
>
> (UNESCO ICH, 2018, chapter 109)

Further, this must be done in a participatory manner that involves practitioners. While the text in no way mentions Open Data or raw data sharing through APIs, it does indicate that data about intangible cultural heritage plays an increasingly important role in heritage management.

While UNESCO conventions are ratified by most countries, they also operate at a level that is perhaps not relevant for the lone heritage professional. Here, local heritage laws, guidelines, traditions or lack of the same come into play. As an example, Denmark has the Archives Act (Bekendtgørelse Af Arkivloven, 2016) and the Museums Act (Bekendtgørelse Af Museumsloven, 2014), as well as laws on repatriation of stolen heritage items, on listed buildings and monuments and on the environment, all of which deal with heritage. The Archives Act establishes how public archives should safeguard the preservation of material heritage value and provides for the discarding of local and national government material that is not deemed worth preservation. It states that public archives must make archival material available to the public, including for research purposes, and must guide citizens on how to use the materials. It also outlines the rules for when materials can be made available to the public and, in particular, when they cannot be. In comparison, the Museums Act is more focused not just on making heritage available but on communicating it in a way that makes it relevant and meaningful for the public.

While reading legal text might not seem like the most obvious route to follow unless you are a lawyer, it can be worthwhile to have a look at the laws governing the heritage area in your country. UNESCO maintains a (not completely up to date) list of national cultural heritage laws. The aim of this database, established in 2003, is to provide a source of information for stakeholders in order to combat the illicit traffic of cultural property (UNESCO, 2019).

The UNESCO database is a good starting point for accessing the laws that are relevant in your country. Some laws may be more straightforward than others. Some may require advice from a local legal expert who can help you to understand how a legal text can be interpreted for your circumstances. There may also be court cases setting precedents where matters are not clearly stated in the laws. The following is a list of questions you can use to examine the legal standing of heritage and OHD in your country.

Questions
- Are there any policies mentioning whether heritage materials can or should be made available to the public?
- Are there any periods of embargo on archival materials?
- Are any public institutions or institution types (e.g. libraries, archives, museums, etc.) charged with preserving, documenting and perhaps making available certain types of heritage materials?
- Are there any legal consequences (e.g. fines, imprisonment) for making certain materials available?

Data protection law

Data protection is not a new issue. However, the extended opportunities to register and share information and data about individuals online have highlighted the issue. Until after the GDPR was approved by the European Parliament on 14 April 2016 (European Union, 2016), I rarely experienced data protection as a topic of discussion and concern in the heritage community. Further, reaction to the GDPR was slow until it was enforced on 25 May 2018. One of the main issues discussed in the heritage community was how to treat the privacy of the deceased. Should we not store or share personal data that can identify people even after they are gone? If so, this would have a huge impact on heritage institutions. This was the concern I heard all around me in Denmark. It was voiced by the chairperson of the Danish Association for Local Archives, Jørgen Thomsen, in December 2018 (Højsgaard, 2018). At the time it still seemed somewhat unclear what provisions had been made for the continued archiving and online publishing of heritage information and portrait photographs of individuals, especially if they were still alive or had died in the preceding ten years. Thomsen argued for a pragmatic approach that neither hinders the collection and registration of heritage nor demotivates the many volunteers working in local archives across Denmark.

Luckily, GDPR makes provisions for heritage, according to the UK Information Commissioner, Elizabeth Denham. 'Data protection law also specifically recognises the importance of archives. There is no inherent conflict with archiving in the public interest; data protection law provides for it through various provisions' (The National Archives, 2018, 4).

The UK National Archives (nationalarchives.gov.uk), together with the UK archives sector, have co-produced a guide to personal archiving where they explain the changes that need to take place in order for archives and other heritage institutions to uphold the new laws. Some of the key points are:

- that individuals now have greater rights over their data, including their right to be forgotten;
- that the law recognises the need for long-term preservation of personal data in the public interest;
- that there are safeguards in place to minimise any adverse impact on living individuals;
- that heritage institutions need to distinguish between processing personal data for the purpose of archiving and for the purposes of daily business;
- that archived personal data can generally be made available to the public once the people concerned have died, or earlier if the use is fair to those concerned.

The GDPR, which all EU member countries had implemented into their own data protection laws by 25 May 2018 states, among other things, that:

> (27) This Regulation does not apply to the personal data of deceased persons. Member States may provide for rules regarding the processing of personal data of deceased persons.
> (50) [...] Further processing for archiving purposes in the public interest, scientific or historical research purposes or statistical purposes should be considered to be compatible lawful processing operations [...]
> (51) [...] The processing of photographs should not systematically be considered to be processing of special categories of personal data as they are covered by the definition of biometric data only when processed through a specific technical means allowing the unique identification or authentication of a natural person. [...]
>
> (European Union, 2016)

The right to be remembered

The idea of the GDPR and data protection laws in general is to protect people – in this case from having their personal data used and misused by others. GDPR describes this as 'the right to be forgotten' (European Union, 2016, Article 17). It states that 'The data subject shall have the right to obtain from the controller the erasure of personal data concerning him or her without undue delay and the controller shall have the obligation to erase personal data without undue delay where one of the following grounds applies' (European Union, 2016, Article 17, paragraph 1). This is followed by a paragraph that states that 'Paragraphs 1 and 2 shall not apply to the extent that processing is necessary ... (d) for archiving purposes in the public interest, scientific or historical research purposes or statistical purposes in accordance with Article 89(1) in so far as the right referred to in paragraph 1 is likely to render impossible or seriously impair the achievement of the objectives of that processing' (European Union, 2016, Article 17, paragraph 3).

In other words, people have the right to have personal data stored about them erased for a number of specified reasons, as long as it is not needed for archiving, scientific or historical research purposes.

An important point in the article on the 'right to be forgotten' is the person's right to actively request to have their data erased. This is not a right that should be wielded by heritage professionals, institutions or other authorities. It should not be used as a tool to forget already marginalised people, deliberately or otherwise. Everyone should also have a right to be remembered. This is where the risk analysis comes in handy again. There must be a balance between general data protection and data diversity.

If we erase or hide the information and stories about marginalised groups in the archives and online, in the long run we are also doing harm to them and the culture and heritage they represent. They will become more invisible, and as a society we will forget that they were there and that their history is perhaps just as long as that of other groups of people.

Questions

1 Does the legal jurisdiction you work within have data protection legislation and, if so, what does it entail?
2 What are the time limits for data protection for archived materials after the death of the person in question?
3 Does the data protection legislation in your country have special provisions for archival and heritage materials?

Copyright law

In essence, copyright is a mechanism to encourage creativity by acknowledging that a person has ownership of works they have created, as well as the sole right to reproduce those works (Cornish, 2015). Copyright generally happens automatically as soon as the work is created and does not need to be registered anywhere (Padfield, 2015).

Basically, copyright is supposed to cover anyone, whether a well known artist or a child, but in reality this depends a lot on the cultural context and in which cases copyright has been tested under different jurisdictions. A few years ago the so-called 'Monkey Selfies' were the centre of a copyright dispute. This case raised the question of authorship, and, so far, the conclusion seems to be that it is reserved for humans (Rosati, 2017). However, some countries, such as Denmark, make a distinction between artistic work and, for example, non-artistic photographs. If something is deemed to be an artistic work the copyright period lasts for 70 years after the death of the creator. However, if it is 'just' a photograph, copyright lasts for only 50 years after it was taken (Bekendtgørelse Af Lov Om Ophavsret, 2014*)*.

Copyright length also varies depending on the jurisdiction. Wikipedia.org keeps an updated list of countries' copyright durations (Wikipedia, 2019a). Most countries in the world have signed the Berne convention (WIPO, 1886), which, among other things, provides a minimum protection period until the expiration of the 50th year after the author's death. Many of these countries (e.g. EU countries and the USA) have chosen to extend this period to Life + 70 years, and a few have gone even further than that, with Mexico providing the longest protection of Life + 100 years.

Further, while copyright generally goes to the creator of the work, some jurisdictions may by default place copyright with an employer. The owner of copyright may also assign the copyright to someone else (Padfield, 2015).

As we have seen, copyright depends on the jurisdiction. However, the Berne Convention operated with the terms 'country of origin' and 'simultaneously published works', which are creating great confusion in online publishing (Fitzgerald et al., 2015). The question arises whether a work published for the first time online originated in the country where the creator is based or in any other country where the work was published simultaneously. This can have consequences for the copyright protection, depending on which jurisdiction is counted as 'country of origin'.

Public domain

As we have seen, copyright does not last forever. After a period of time (usually 50 or 70 years after the death of the creator) copyright runs out and the works are then in the public domain. Again, this is dependent on the jurisdiction and online publication can cause complications here. Being in the public domain means that the work is no longer protected by copyright and can be reused by the public.

In the heritage sector there are vast amounts of material that are in the public domain, which in essence means that they could be open to the public. However, most institutions around the world simply do not have the resources to enable this on a massive scale and many do not have the inclination to do so, for a variety of reasons (as discussed earlier in the chapter). Another issue is posed by institutions that claim copyright of digital reproductions of works in the public domain as a fund-raising strategy (Petri, 2014) – especially, if they, as holders of those works, restrict others from sharing reproductions of the said public domain works. Under UK jurisdiction this process depends on whether the reproduction of the original work meets the threshold of originality in order to be protected by copyright (Hamilton and Saunderson, 2017, 72). While this threshold is more difficult to reach for a reproduction of a two-dimensional work, it may be easier if the original work is a 3D piece.

However, a counter culture can be found in the Free Culture Movement and the OpenGLAM principles:

> Keep digital representations of works for which copyright has expired (public domain) in the public domain by not adding new rights to them.
>
> (OpenGLAM, 2019, Principle 2)

Even though it may be legal to claim copyright on an original photograph taken of a 3D artwork in the public domain (Pekel, 2014), this is not encouraged, for ethical reasons.

Free culture licensing

The Creative Commons (CC) licensing scheme is based on the idea of balance between encouraging creative innovation and protecting the innovators. It began in 2001 with the support of the Center for the Public Domain, and taking inspiration from the Free Software Foundation's GNU General Public License (Creative Commons, 2011).

> Our legal tools help those who want to encourage reuse of their works by offering them for use under generous, standardized terms; those who want to make creative uses of works; and those who want to benefit from this symbiosis. Our vision is to help others realize the full potential of the internet.
>
> (Creative Commons, 2019a)

There currently exists six different CC licences with legal text that is both human and machine readable. These include a combination of one or more of the following elements:

- BY: requires attribution to the creator (is included in all six licences);
- NC: prohibits commercial use of the material;
- ND: prohibits the sharing of adaptations;
- SA: requires adaptations of the material be released under the same licence. (Creative Commons, 2019b)

The overall idea of CC is that it is a tool which, through a series of questions, identifies the right combination of licensing elements.[4] The most open licence is CC BY, meaning that the work can be reused in any way, as long as the creator is attributed. The least open licence is CC BY-NC-ND, meaning that the work must be attributed, cannot be used commercially and may not be distributed in a modified form (Creative Commons, 2019b). In addition to this, CC provides licensing text and tools to mark works in the public domain and works for which the user wants to waive all rights (CC0).

However, two elements of the CC licences have proved to be problematic, despite the initial wish to provide tools for the free sharing of culture. First is the NC or Non-Commercial element, which states that a work cannot be used in a way deemed commercial. As we have previously discussed (Chapter 1) commercial use in itself is difficult to define on the internet. Second is the ND or Non-Derivative licence, which prevents reuse and further creativity building on the original work. Further, an -ND or -NC licence makes the work incompatible with one of the most visited culture-sharing platforms in the world, Wikipedia (Freedom Defined, 2017). Only works that are freely licensed (or in the public domain) can be shared on Wikipedia: CC0, CC BY and CC BY-SA.

In 2019 Andrea Wallace and Douglas McCarthy set out to study GLAM open access policy and practice through a web survey (McCarthy and Wallace, 2019). They found that while the most commonly used open licence for digital surrogates was the Public Domain Mark (36.8%), CC licenses (CC BY-SA, CC BY and CC0) make up nearly 50% of the licences used in total (McCarthy, 2019).

Orphan works

Orphan works are works that are thought to be protected by copyright but for which the creator cannot be identified or found. Because copyright protection in many countries lasts for 70 years after the death of the creator, heritage institutions have increasingly large amounts of material in copyright, and a large proportion of these do not have identified creators. The British Library, for example, estimates that 40% of their print works are orphaned. This poses huge issues for institutions and users alike, as well as for creators (Lifshitz-Goldberg, 2010).

It is a lose-lose situation where institutions cannot publish relevant heritage material, works and creators lie forgotten in the archives and users miss out on creative opportunities.

Depending on the jurisdiction, dealing with orphan works ranges from difficult to near impossible. Some countries, such as Canada and Hungary, provide a licensing scheme where, after a reasonable search for the copyright holder, users can apply to an official entity for a licence and pay a determined licence fee. Other countries, such as Norway, Denmark and the Netherlands, have a collective licence mechanism whereby users, for example institutions, can obtain a general licence for a central body to use any copyrighted material in their work (Lifshitz-Goldberg, 2010). Nevertheless, both options create extra work and/or cost for users, who could be excused for choosing the path of least resistance and turning their backs on orphan works.

One user who chose to follow the orphan works licensing path is Melissa Terras, Professor in Digital Heritage at the University of Edinburgh, who in 2014 decided to test the new UK regulations for orphan works as well as the UK Intellectual Property Office's licence application system. Terras's award-winning blog post (Terras, 2014) about this process is at the same time interesting, funny and extremely frustrating. It illustrates perfectly the difficulty of obtaining licences for orphan works and exemplifies how the way copyright law is implemented today is very much at odds with both heritage and creativity.

What I have tried to illustrate here is that copyright is by no means simple. In fact, I suspect that there are many people making a good living on the premise that copyright is complicated. Again, the fear of getting it wrong means that many heritage institutions may choose to play safe. But the risk of low societal impact and funding cuts must be weighed against the risk of a copyright failure. Perhaps some of these latter risks can be reduced through better knowledge about copyright and licensing.

Questions

1 Has your country signed the Berne Convention, and how long is copyright protection in your country?
2 Is copyright the same for all works, or does your country have different copyright terms for artistic works, different media types or databases?
3 How are free culture licences, public domain and orphan works handled in your country?
4 Are there any larger institutions in your country that you can look to for inspiration and guidance on how to deal with copyright and online publishing?

Summary

This chapter has:

1 discussed the frustration and risk connected with a lack of knowledge about legal issues faced by the heritage sector in relation to open data;
2 exemplified heritage laws on both an international and a national level, with a specific focus on provisions for data sharing;
3 discussed data protection laws, among others the EU GDPR, and how they can work with and against open heritage;
4 discussed the essence of copyright and the issues surrounding heritage collections, such as licensing, orphan works and re-appropriation of works in the public domain;
5 posed questions at the end of each section to help readers to identify important elements of laws that apply in their jurisdiction.

Notes

1   Advice given by Michael Edson, then Director of Web and New Media Strategy at the Smithsonian Institute, to the SMK in 2011 at a time where they were reconsidering their image licensing policy for their online collections. (Sanderhoff, 2017)
2   As of 31 January 2017, 193 countries, including 189 United Nations member states as well as the Cook Islands, the Holy See, Niue and the State of Palestine, but excluding four United Nations member states: Liechtenstein, Nauru, Somalia and Tuvalu.
3   With only 178 state parties, not including Australia, Canada, USA and the UK.
4   See Hamilton and Saunderson (2017) for more on open licensing in the heritage sector.

Publishing open data

Heritage data can take many forms, from digitised oil paintings to lists of archaeological finds. Thus, there is no one-size-fits-all solution to publishing these many varied data forms.

The aim of this chapter is to ensure that professionals and amateurs in the heritage community, such as museum curators, archivists, community historians, etc. can get practical advice and inspiration on how to publish their own datasets. The examples used are taken from around the world to show the varying degree of openness in publishing OHD today.

I will use the five questions from the OHD Model explained in Chapter 1 to evaluate the openness of the published data in each example.

1 Is the material published online, with metadata so that it can be searched and filtered?
2 Is the material published with an open licence or in the public domain, and is this clearly communicated in conjunction with the material?
3 Does the institution actively encourage reuse of the material and provide support for anyone who wishes to reuse it, free of charge?
4 Is the material available in an open, machine-readable format that anyone can export/download?
5 Is the material available through a well-described web service or API that anyone has access to?

Each of these questions opens up for further questions, which will be exemplified in the following. For example, if heritage collections are published online with metadata, this opens them up for a basic discovery of what the collections contain. This discovery is usually independent of location and can lead to further interest in the institution in question. However, an important aspect of the metadata can be whether the material is accessible to view at the institution. For example, is the artwork on display, or is it possible to read the documents?

If the material is published with open licences or the institution communicates clearly that it is in the public domain, which parts of the material are covered? Does the CC0 licence cover the only metadata provided by the institution, and which images are in or out of copyright?

If the institution encourages reuse, how do they communicate this to users? Sometimes this is written only on an 'about' page, meaning that the users have to go looking in order to learn that the material is available for reuse. Other times, institutions make this information clear for each item, for example with a 'use this image' button.

If the material is available to download in an open, machine-readable format it is again important to be clear about who can use the files and for what purpose. Is it for research and non-commercial use only? Since batch downloads are usually static files, it is important to ensure that users know when the material was compiled and whether they can expect an update.

If the material is available through an API it is very important that this is well described. Quick-start guides with example URLs are always a good idea if the institution is looking to encourage the use of their API; for example, how the URL would look for a simple search of the collection. Here it is also important that the documentation makes it clear how to find images, choose rights, choose data format, etc. in their search URL.

The following sections are divided into the different institutions within the GLAM sector: galleries (i.e. art museums), libraries, archives and museums. There is certainly some overlap between the materials that are published as open data in these different institutions. All have some sort of collection which is often published online with images of each item. Nevertheless, this is primarily exemplified in the section on galleries, as the material here is almost exclusively visual and published as images with metadata. Some libraries make the content of books and newspapers available as digitised images and full text. Archives often have lists of people who can be searched for – for example in census records, passenger lists, etc. This type of material is very popular among family historians and has led to collaboration with large commercial or non-profit family history companies. Museums often have collections of objects that can be published as images in a similar way to the art published by galleries. Some museums have material that is geographically located and can be published on a map. Finally, many heritage institutions choose to publish their material through a collaborative GLAM portal on top of or instead of their own website. These GLAM portals are usually just collections of metadata and media (e.g. images, video, audio) but will often link back to the original institution's collection, if such is available.

Galleries/art museums

When the Dutch Rijksmuseum began to make high-resolution images of their masterpieces available online in 2011–13 they 'argued that the core goal of the museum is to get the public familiar with their collection, and that the internet can greatly facilitate that' (Pekel, 2014, 7). Open data was seen as a means to entice the public to visit the museum, rather than as an alternative to a museum visit.

For many non-commercial galleries or art museums[1] the collections have a clear monetary value and therefore many have or have had a commercial practice of selling digital copies of these works. It is therefore understandable that art museums will fear a loss of revenue when giving open access to their collections – in particular, revenue from commercial use of their images. However, whether something has a commercial use is not easy to determine. This is one of the reasons why Freedom Defined's definition of 'free cultural works' does not include non-commercial clauses. They say: 'Many bloggers and blog communities on the web use advertising as a way to recoup costs and generate income. [...] Ask yourself if you really want to stop all these individuals from using your work' (Freedom Defined, 2017).

The staff at the Los Angeles County Museum of Art (lacma.org) felt that making the decision between what is commercial and what is not, as well as monitoring commercial use, was becoming so difficult that they decided to make high-resolution images of the parts of their collection that were in the public domain freely available online for all purposes in 2013 (Kelly, Council on Library and Information Resources, and Andrew W. Mellon Foundation, 2013).

There are many methods available for publishing images that are open and accessible. We will start by looking at a method that is very popular and allows access to the images but does not allow reuse. It can answer yes to the first OHD question: 'Is the material published online, with metadata so that it can be searched and found?' Art Museum of Estonia Digital Collection (kunstimuuseum.ekm.ee) is one such example. The collection enables users to search the entire collection by artist name, work title, keywords and collection number as well as to filter by predefined categories, collections and a list of artists. A search for 'botanical' returns seven images, among them a painting by Linda Kits-Mägi (1916–90) called *In the Greenhouse of the Botanical Garden of the State University of Tartu* (1947). The metadata describes the painting as oil on canvas, 82 x 101 cm, with further details provided in Estonian. It makes visible the art of Kits-Mägi and other artists in the collection for anyone who is interested in it. However, apart from finding them, reading about them and perhaps downloading them individually, there is not much else one can do with the images in this collection. It is unclear whether the museum claims copyright of the image or whether copyright is vested in the estate of Kits-Mägi. Looking through the collection, it seems that the museum also claims copyright over images of art from the 15th century, so it is tempting to conclude that, instead of making the actual copyright status of each artwork clear, the museum has just added a blanket copyright to stop reuse in general.

Other institutions have similar online collections, but instead of blanket statements claiming that copyright belongs to the museum they display the actual copyright of the images/original artwork and make sure to also publish images that have open licences or are in the public domain. An example of this is the Art Institute of Chicago, USA (artic.edu). Like the Art Museum of Estonia's digital collection, it provides ample possibilities for doing a free-text search as well as filtering on artist. It is also possible to filter by type of artwork and medium, dates, subject and, most importantly, whether a work is in the public domain. Further, against each item in the collection its copyright status is clearly stated and there is a link to a page explaining the Institute's open access policy.

The Rijksmuseum have taken their collection a step further and have developed the Rijksstudio application. This is meant to encourage reuse of the collection in a very extensive way. Once you have an account, you can create your own sets of artwork.

For example, I have created a set called 'Botanical drawings' where I can collect illustrations of flowers in a particular style that I like. To find the first image for my set I initially searched on 'botanical' and was quite disappointed with the result. However, one artwork was appropriate, and after adding that to my set I could scroll down and see other sets, created by other users, that included this artwork. These sets also contained other artworks that I would like for my set on 'Botanical drawings', and thus I could continue my browsing of the collections via the sets made by my fellow users (Figure 3.1 opposite). This function is similar to the visual inspiration-gathering site Pinterest.com in the way you can use other people's collections (i.e. Pinterest boards) to find more images for your own boards.

The Metropolitan Museum of Art, New York, USA (The Met; metmuseum.org) have made their artwork available, through their online collection, to be searched and filtered in a similar manner to that described above. You can search and filter the results according to whether they are open access. Each artwork is clearly labelled with its licence and is available through the collection API as well as the website.

The search that is available through the Met's open access API is not as extensive as the search options in the online collection: there are no filtering options, but only a free-text search using two separate methods to retrieve

Figure 3.1 *Screenshot from Rijksstudio (rijksmuseum.nl) showing other recent collections/sets with the artwork 'Scabiosa', Anonymous, 1688–98, public domain*

data from the Met's open access dataset, and images of individual pieces of artwork. The user first must access the 'Search' option and enter the search term, which in the following example is 'sunflower':

```
https://collectionapi.metmuseum.org/public/collection/v1/search?q=sunflowers
```

The result is a JSON formatted list of all the object IDs (identifiers) of the artworks that match the search term. If the user or application wants to access the object data for each of the artworks in the list they must use the 'Object' search, together with the object ID of the artwork, which in this case is 436524:[2]

```
https://collectionapi.metmuseum.org/public/collection/v1/objects/436524
```

The reply to this request returns the dataset for the artwork *Sunflowers* by Vincent van Gogh (1887), including a link to a high-resolution digital image of the public domain work, the medium (oil on canvas), the dimensions (17 x 24 in. (43.2 x 61 cm)) and information about the artist, all in the machine-readable format JSON. All the artworks available in the Met's open access dataset are in the public domain and the metadata for each image is made available by the Met under the CC0 licence, meaning that the Met has waived all copyright to the dataset (see Chapter 2 for more on licensing).

This exemplifies how some art museums have developed their own online collections and made them available using varying degrees of openness. The Art Museum of Estonia can answer in the positive to question 1 of the OHD Model, as their collection is published online with metadata and can be searched and filtered. However, it is not clear in their collection which images are under copyright and which are in the public domain. In the next collection, from the Art Institute of Chicago, this is made clear for each artwork and explained on a specific page. The Rijksmuseum not only make the copyright status of artworks in their collections clear but also facilitate active reuse through the RijkStudio, where users can curate their own collections and are encouraged to download images and create physical copies of artworks. Finally, The Met have made artworks in their collection that are in the public domain available through an API, as well as via an online collection. This makes their dataset available for even further reuse as a whole, and not just the individual digital images. They can then be used for apps, tools and research, which I will explain further in Chapters 5–7.

However, what happens to art museums that do not have the resources or interest to make their collections available online via a bespoke search engine? The Art Museums of Skagen (skagenskunstmuseer.dk), Denmark are one such example. They are based in Skagen, at the northernmost tip of Denmark, where the seas of Kattegat and Skagerrak meet. Skagen is famous on account of the special quality of its natural light and the artists who flocked to the area in the late 19th century. While many of these artists have been dead for over 70 years, which is when copyright expires in Denmark, the museum does not make any of their collection available for reuse online. In fact, the only page on the museum's website that mentions copyright is the page for ordering photographs, against a fee. On this page the museum, like the Art Museum of Estonia, claims copyright over the digital reproduction of all their artwork. However, despite the lack of online publication the museum does use other platforms to publish certain parts of their collection. For example, they have used the photograph-sharing platform Flickr to publish an album of 163 photographs from the Art Colony at Skagen, which are shared using the CC BY-SA licence.

Another Danish art museum, the Hirschsprung Collection (hirschsprung. dk), also does not have an online, searchable collection. However, the part of their collection that is in the public domain is available on Wikipedia.

The advantage of using existing platforms such as Flickr.com and Wikipedia.org is that the museum does not need to develop its own, for which many museums do not have the resources. Further, many of these platforms are developed for image and knowledge sharing and thus have built in APIs as well as an established viewership. Both these platforms also require the user to be clear on the copyright status of images before uploading them, which means that museums have to make decisions about each image before they publish them.

Libraries

Libraries have a long history of shared standards for cataloguing, and the creation of the MAchine Readable Cataloguing (MARC) standard in the 1960s enabled cross-library data sharing of bibliographic data (Elings and Waibel, 2007). These very structured library catalogues are in most cases available for online searching. For example, the National Library of Norway (nb.no) has made their collections available for searching and filtering online. However, access to digitised books depends on where the user is based and what the rights for the material are. Some material (approx. 30,000) is freely available for all users, while all books published in Norway up to the year 2000 (approx. 215,000) can be freely accessed online from a Norwegian IP (Internet Protocol) address and digitised Norwegian books from 2001 onwards (approx. 450,000) can be accessed locally at the National Library.

Harvard Library, USA (library.harvard.edu) is an example of a library that has provided open access to their bibliographic metadata through a live API, the Harvard LibraryCloud. The API is well described and gives access to over 20 million metadata records that can be retrieved in the Metadata Object Description Schema or the Dublin Core (DC) standard, using the data formats XML or JSON.

```
https://api.lib.harvard.edu/v2/items.dc.json?q=botanical
```

Information on how to format the URL illustrated here is provided on the API page, giving outsiders easy access to the API. The first part of the URL (https://api.lib.harvard.edu/v2/) calls the API. The DC standard and JSON data format are then specified and the search term (q=botanical) is sent. This returns the first ten (default is 10, limit is 250, pagination is possible, see Chapter 5 for more on this) results from the catalogue that are relevant to the search term 'botanical'.

The reason why Harvard Library does this is that it has an open metadata policy which makes its metadata available for public use under the CC0 licence.

The Library of Congress, USA (loc.gov) has tried to publish their digital collections as open data in machine-readable formats. However, while these digital collections and their access points are shared on the web page 'LC for Robots', it is not quite clear what data is available through the different APIs and bulk data downloads. For example, the MARC records of 25 million records in the collection are available to download as UTF-8 (Unicode Transformation Format 8-bit), MARC8 or XML. However, when you look more closely the 2016 records are available to buy, while it is the 2014 retrospective file sets that are available as open data. Library of Congress has further made some collections available through APIs, although this 'does not include records from the library catalogue'. The digital collection's API is a work in progress and is not very well documented. Nevertheless, the separate API for the Library of Congress newspaper collection, Chronicling America (chroniclingamerica.loc.gov), is easy to use and the newspapers available here are all believed to be in the public domain.

```
https://chroniclingamerica.loc.gov/search/pages/results/?andtext=botanical&
format=json
```

The URL illustrated here for a simple search of mentions of the text 'botanical' in the format JSON returns the default 20 results of newspaper articles that include the word on the page. The first result returned is from *The Day Book*, Chicago, 1917 bearing the title 'Women farmers will be carpenters, too'. The text 'botanical' is in the caption, which is searchable because the newspaper images have been converted to text through Optical Character Recognition (OCR). As is shown in Figure 3.2, this is not a 100% accurate system, resulting in extra characters and errors. However, it is, a powerful tool and today one of the only realistic options for the automated reading of millions of lines of text like those we find in old newspapers.

WOMEN FARMERS WILL BE CARPENTERS, TOO
Before being fullfledged fanners
women must be able to make the ne
cessary tools and utensils for the
farm. A group is here shown, in the
New York botanical garden school
for women, making garden boxes.

Figure 3.2 *Newspaper clipping from The Day Book, Chicago, 23 April 1917 (public domain), with the search text 'botanical' marked and the OCR below. From Chronicling America, Library of Congress (chroniclingamerica.loc.gov)*

Apart from bibliographical catalogues, many libraries have books and other text and non-text materials in their collections that have been digitised. The University of British Columbia (UBC), Canada, Library Open Collections is an example of this.

UBC has a digital collection (open.library.ubc.ca) of British Columbia historical books that they make available for searching and viewing with related metadata and full text. For example, a search for historical books with the term 'botanical' returned 396 books. The term can be found on many different pages of the book *Autobiography of John Macoun, M.A.: Canadian explorer and naturalist, assistant director and naturalist to the Geological Survey of Canada, 1831–1920*. The open collections platform lets the user see a list of the 396 results, and for each result there is a quick view of the first ten instances of the search term. The book itself can be read in the online portal and can be downloaded as a whole with the original pages in a PDF, or as full-text in a .txt document.

The book was published in 1922 by the Ottawa Field-Naturalists' Club, but whether or not the book, images, metadata or its full text of the book are in the public domain and can be freely reused is unclear. The metadata for the book states that the images can be used for reference and research only.

It is also possible to explore the UBC historical book collection by genre, or on a timeline that begins in 1776 with 'Summary observations and facts collected from late and authentic accounts of Russian and other navigators'. This collection, along with the other open collections at UBC, is also available to search and reuse through an API, where again it is not entirely clear what rights there are for reuse.

Examples above have illustrated how libraries have made their collections available online for the general world public. Some, like the National Library of Norway, provide different levels of access depending on whether the user is in Norway or not. Others, like UBC, make everything available to search and view, but reuse is limited to reference and research. Libraries not only make their bibliographic catalogues available but also provide access to other digitised material from their catalogue, such as the newspapers in the Library of Congress Chronicling America collection.

Archives

Archives often have large amounts of unstructured material in their collections, like documents, private letters, pictures, maps, as well as more structured material such as passenger lists, census records, church and civil registration. This section will focus on the latter type. Other institutions have lists and structured data that can be published in similar ways.

Because of their heterogeneous holdings of materials, it can be rather difficult to develop a systematic register and digitisation effort for an archive's collections. Instead, it is often easier to digitise and publish particular collections as individual projects. Much archived material has been created by governments or private individuals and companies, but has not been published in the same way as a book, or created by an artist. Therefore, it can be difficult to determine the copyright status of materials, which is one of the key components of open data. Further, much of the structured datasets in archives provides names and perhaps other identifiable information about individuals, which means that data protection laws need to be taken into consideration.

The Danish Demographic Database (DDD; ddd.dda.dk), a part of the Danish National Archives, is an example of a large collection of census records that have been transcribed by volunteers since 1992 and have been published online in a searchable manner since 1996. The dataset is made freely available for anyone to use. The National Archives states that they do not control how the data is used, but nowhere on the site do they make it clear which copyright restrictions cover the material. The dataset is mainly used by family researchers, who add the census records to their own family tree databases. However, this enormous dataset is not available as machine-readable data in a way that makes it reusable for other purposes.

This did not stop Danish-born Marianne and Dan Nicolaysen, now living in Australia, from creating a new online database system using the dataset from DDD. They imported and cleaned the dataset from DVD versions released by the Danish National Archives in 2011. After they received permission from the National Archives, the online database went live in 2013 as Danish Family Search (DFS; danishfamilysearch.dk). The Nicolaysens say that DFS is the largest crowdsourcing project in Denmark, with 26,309 active members[3] and approximately 6600 new names recorded in the database daily (D. Nicolaysen, personal communication, 2019).

Archives New Zealand (archives.govt.nz) similarly aims some of their digital collections at family historians, for example the searchable passenger lists from 1839 to 1973. These are lists of outbound and inbound passengers going through the ports of New Zealand, including airplane arrivals to Auckland between 1939 and 1965. This collection is published through the FamilySearch site, where it is freely available once you sign up to a free FamilySearch account. Here the original lists have been indexed so they can be searched for some information (i.e. names, dates, places, ship names), while digital copies of the originals are available to view and download.

The National Archives in the UK provides open access to search their collections both through an online service called Discovery as well as through the Discovery API. However, this provides access to only the metadata. For some of the digitised datasets heavily watermarked preview image is available, and the documents/images themselves can be downloaded for a fee or viewed for free at The National Archives in Kew, London. This despite the items' status of 'Public Record(s)'.

The US National Archives, on the other hand, offers a similar combination of online collection and collection API for their items, which are accessible as images for free. They are further marked as 'unrestricted access' and 'unrestricted use', meaning that not only can they be viewed in the collection but they are also available for reuse. This is a part of the National Archives' measure to implement the Open Data Policy of 9 May 2013 (Obama, 2013).

While the above examples make available digitised versions of heritage material or the metadata thereof, another large archiving task today is the preservation of all the material on the internet that is becoming a part of our heritage. The Internet Archive (archive.org) is a non-profit organisation with headquarters in San Francisco, USA and data centres around the world to back up their data. The Internet Archive began archiving the web in 1996, making it available to the public in 2001 through the Wayback Machine. Today the archive consists of 330 billion web pages that can be navigated using a timeline of captures and which are available to search and browse freely for 'researchers, historians, scholars, the print disabled and the general public' (Internet Archive, 2019).

Museums

Art museums are discussed above in the section on galleries, and while many other types of museum have similar collections that can be published online with images and metadata, they also sometimes have other materials, for example geographical material, that must be displayed differently. This section will provide examples of both.

The Smithsonian Institution (si.edu) is the world's largest museum complex, consisting of 19 museums and the United States National Zoo. There are 154 million objects in the Smithsonian's collections, of which 14 million are available online as digital records. These online records can be searched and filtered via either the Collections Search Centre or the newer-looking Explore Interests portal, which is accessible from the Smithsonian front page. Both search engines seem to find similar material in a search for the term 'botanical'. The result includes approximately 40,000 museum objects relevant to botany, with metadata and sometimes images. However, it is not clear in either of these search engines whether any of the metadata or media is available for reuse. In most heritage collections which do not consist of art or published materials it is very difficult to determine who created an item. Further, many museum collections include specimens or everyday objects that, as such, are not created and are therefore not under copyright. In such cases it is usually the museum's digital photograph of the object that is copyrighted and the museum or the photographer that holds the copyright (see Chapter 2). In order to make these objects available to view online the museum can publish the digital images or the objects under a Creative Commons licence or in the public domain. On their Terms of Use page the Smithsonian states that the content is identified as having 'no known copyright restrictions'. Because copyright is difficult to determine for most of their material 'the Smithsonian makes its content available for personal and non-commercial educational uses consistent with the principles of fair use' (Smithsonian, 2019).

The UK Science Museum Group (sciencemuseumgroup.org.uk) also makes their collections available online to search and filter. For each item in the collection the rights and usage of all content is made very clear according to the following:

- Data in the title, made, maker and details fields: Creative Commons Zero
- Descriptions and all other text content: Creative Commons Attribution 4.0 licence
- Imagery and photography: the licensing and copyright varies per image (please check the source.legal.rights.usage for each image).

(Science Group Museum, 2019)

In other words, object metadata is free of any restrictions and can be used by anyone for any purpose. Any text descriptions can be used for any purpose but should be attributed to the Science Museum Group. However, images are licensed differently and copyright for photographs of objects is attributed to the Board of Trustees of the Science Museum, London, who have published them under a Creative Commons Attribution-NonCommercial-ShareAlike (CC BY-NC-SA) licence. This is also the case for faithful digital reproductions of drawings where the maker has been dead for over 70 years and where the original drawing would be in the public domain.

Auckland Museum (aucklandmuseum.com) in New Zealand has similarly made their collection of objects available through 'Collections Online'. Through this site it is possible to search the item's metadata and view images of parts of the collection. For example, a search for 'botanical' returns 11,606 records, of which 8425 have images, and of these 2617 can be downloaded and reused. All objects found in the collection can be added to a feature called 'My Collection', which disappears once you leave the site but can be saved and accessed via a link. In other words, you can make collections of objects without logging into an account. These collections, along with the search results and individual items, can be exported as a CSV file and accessed through the Auckland Museum API.

These examples have all shown museums that make objects in their collections available with varying degrees of openness. However, for some museum collections geographical location is an important part of the object metadata. The following is an example of a site that makes geographical heritage data available both for online searching and viewing, as well as through an API.

The Open Context site (opencontext.org) is administered by the Alexandria Archive Institute, a non-profit company operating out of the USA and run by Sarah and Eric Kansa. The site provides publication options for research data mainly from archaeological projects and field work. All data is published using CC licences so that it is enabled for reuse. A search for 'botanical' returns 17 results plotted on the map (Figure 3.3) and in list form. This same data is available through the Open Context API, which returns data in both the JSON format and the GeoJSON format, which is aimed at geospatial data structures.

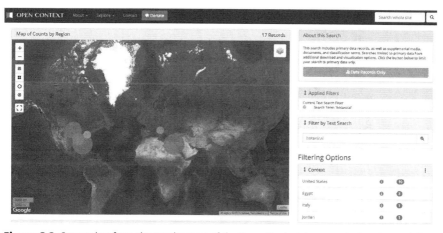

Figure 3.3 *Screenshot from the results map of the Open Context (opencontext.org) search for 'botanical'*

Finally, geographical data can also be shared through government open data portals, often using the format GeoJSON. An example of this is the openAfrica portal (africaopendata.org), which aims to be the largest independent repository of open data on the African continent. The data is collected by volunteers and a few organisations, and here it is possible to find GeoJSON datasets on, for example, protected areas. These are not published as curated and visualised datasets in the same way that we see in Open Context. Rather, they allow a simple search for full and often static datasets that can then be downloaded or accessed via a static URL in code form (see Chapter 5 for an example of how to visualise this type of data on a map).

GLAM

This chapter has so far presented different ways of publishing open data online, divided into different cultural institution types: galleries, libraries, archives and museums. This final section will show how heritage material is sometimes published across institutions with a mix of material types and with other features.

Finna (finna.fi) is a national resource with free search access to materials from Finnish museums, libraries and archives, which is evolving to replace single-institution user interfaces. The platform enables a search across books, art, texts, maps, sounds and more that can be read online, as well as the option to log in and place a reservation on books and other materials through the library system.

Because Finna enables a search of material from across more than 300 organisations, permission to use different materials like images and books varies. In general, images on the site include a copyright statement. The terms of service state that descriptions about materials on the Finna site can be freely used, with the exception of material under third-party copyright (e.g. from publishers or Finna users). While there are no open licenses to be found, they do however include an API that allows outside users to search the dataset and retrieve results in a JSON format.

Two big players in GLAM portals are Europeana (europeana.eu) and Digital Public Library of America (DPLA; dp.la). Each aims to connect people to materials held in GLAM institutions across their jurisdiction, with a special focus on education. Both act as searchable portals to millions of records, and work to mediate the materials and stories relevant to their region.

DPLA, for example, does this through a series of online exhibitions that, unfortunately, are not linked to the metadata in the collection, as well as primary source sets on various themes, where the material is linked to the records in DPLA. Europeana has a similar series of online exhibitions, where the materials are linked to their original records in Europeana or elsewhere. Further, Europeana has created thematic collections that change over time as more and more materials become available. For example, there is an archaeology collection where it is possible to search a subsection of over two million records.

These large portals contain vast amounts of materials, and have the authority of being backed by thousands of organisations. This in turn enables them to combine materials into pan-European or pan-American narratives. At the same time their institutional and parliamentary backing makes them important actors in the political landscape of heritage, with resources at their disposal that enable them to publish open datasets with a confidence that is difficult to find elsewhere. Each of these two portals has a professional community and a 'pro' site where they mediate their content to, among others, educators and developers.

Europeana educational resources include apps built on the collections, options for partnerships and community, as well as a thoroughly documented API. The latter have various entry points, like a simple search or record API, an IIIF (International Image Interoperability Framework) API tailored to display newspaper materials and specialised services like SPARQL, OAI-PMH (Open Archives Initiative Protocol for Metadata Harvesting), or LOD. Further, Europeana contributes to open data by providing the EDM (Europeana Data Model), a standard, based on existing institutional standards, that enables interoperability across institutional datasets through mapping to this common data model.

The DPLA 'pro' site provides educational resources in a similar way to Europeana, with a clear focus on access to primary sources on American history. It includes resources for researchers and developers, such as the option for bulk download for research purposes, as well as a very clearly documented API with a nifty 'cheat sheet' to get you started. Their philosophy about the API is to 'encourage the independent development of applications, tools, and resources that make use of data contained in the DPLA platform in new and innovative ways, from anywhere, at any time' (DPLA, 2019). Another DPLA philosophy that comes across in their API is that they make use of existing community standards and open source technology in an attempt not to reinvent the wheel.

The great advantage of these portals is that they provide both an interface and a data entry point to materials from institutions that do not necessarily provide all these things themselves. An example is the American Smithsonian Institute, whose interface was introduced earlier in this chapter. The Smithsonian at this time only has a limited API for American art, while the DPLA provides the option of accessing data from other Smithsonian collections through their API.

These portals further educate and encourage other smaller institutions in sharing heritage data in an open manner. Europeana has a Data Exchange Agreement structuring the relationship between the portal and its data providers. This establishes two main rules related to intellectual property rights for the metadata and content delivered to Europeana:

1 All metadata submitted to Europeana will be published as open data under the terms of the Creative Commons Zero Public Domain Dedication (CC0).
2 Each digital object (which includes the associated preview) that is available via Europeana needs to carry a rights statement that describes its copyright status. If an object is in the public domain, it must be labelled as being in the public domain.

(Europeana, 2015)

GLAM portals thus come in different sizes, from national portals covering a single country to international portals covering a larger region. However, because of the heterogeneous materials from across the GLAM sector, these portals often provide access only to basic metadata, and perhaps images.

Summary

This chapter has:

1 explored various methods for publishing heritage data among GLAM institutions online, using the five questions from the OHD Model to evaluate the different degrees of openness;
2 illustrated how galleries/art museums publish images and image metadata. This section also provides an introduction and some inspiration for other institution types that want to publish images and other document formats like video and audio that require publication alongside metadata;
3 illustrated how libraries publish full-text documents, for example texts that have been scanned and digitised using OCR, such as newspapers. These publication methods can also be used for texts that are born digital (e.g. blog posts) or that have been transcribed from handwriting (e.g. historic documents or letters);
4 illustrated how archives publish structured materials and records (e.g. census records or passenger lists). These methods can also be used for other material in structured form, for example archaeological lists of finds, or an art museum's list of purchases;
5 illustrated how museums publish their collections of items, which is similar to the publication of images and metadata as covered in the galleries section. These items can also include geographical locations,

which can be published in a map form, as was exemplified for archaeological material;

6 illustrated how many different heritage materials from the GLAM sector can be published through cross-institutional portals covering either a single country or a larger region. The type of data published through these portals is often limited to images (or other document types), metadata and links to the institutions' records where more information can sometimes be found.

Notes

1 A gallery in the context of GLAM institutions should not be confused with a commercial gallery. The term can be used as a synonym for an art museum; for example, many countries have a national gallery as the nation's foremost art museum.

2 Object 436524 is *Sunflowers*, 1887, Vincent van Gogh.

3 As of 30 October 2019.

## 4

Using and reusing open data

Heritage is not static. It is continually developing and redeveloping, combining and splitting, alongside or together with current cultural trends. In essence this means that we are all using heritage and heritage material in our lives, whether through a modern Ikea table inspired by century-old designs or a family heirloom that we have painstakingly restored. We introduce our children to our own favourite childhood characters. We interpret current politics based on what we know and understand about the history of the world around us. Our heritage is with us in our daily lives and in our interactions with other people. It is all around us and can be tangible or intangible, or a combination of both. Heritage that is tangible is what we can see and touch. It is the type that is often displayed in museums or accessed in archives. Intangible heritage comes to light in songs, performances, oral stories, and is much more difficult to quantify. It is also present in datasets through transcriptions, recordings or videos, as well as maps and more. Intangible heritage can be recorded with technology and published as datasets that can be shared alongside tangible heritage datasets.

Nonetheless, we are not able to use heritage that we do not know about: heritage that is forgotten, or lost, or even just hidden in archives and in dusty lofts. The first requirement for heritage to be used and reused is for it to be available. The previous chapters have focused on making heritage available. This chapter will look at what is possible and what can happen when heritage and heritage material are made available in an open manner.

Readers can use this chapter as an inspirational catalogue that showcases different examples of use and reuse of heritage and heritage data.

Use and users

One of the first issues to tackle with heritage data use and reuse is that of the users themselves. Before any online publication of a heritage collection, it is vital to examine who the users could be and what uses they might have for the data. Terras (2015b) has examined the various ways that reuse of digitised heritage content has been studied through both qualitative and quantitative measures, and acknowledges the difficulty in doing so. Often the seemingly simple act of gathering statistics and reports on how digitised collections have been used is thwarted by the short-term and underfunded nature of such projects.

Further, the notion of who may use heritage data is in constant flux. In a report on the use and users of data from the US National Archives and Records Administration (NARA), Adams (2007) found that there are two primary groups of users. The first and main user type in the 20th century was academics, using raw datasets for original research. When the report was written in 2007 the tide had changed and 'information-seeking users' now far outnumbered the former. Their focus was on finding specific factual or personal information in the archives. This shift towards larger user groups using online heritage collections as information sources in their personal projects (e.g. family history) should have a huge influence on how heritage collections are published. Lessons learnt in the 21st century show that we cannot afford an attitude of 'if you build it they will come'. Instead, we would do well to learn from some of both the smaller and larger heritage collections online that specifically engage with 'information-seeking users' (e.g. family history platforms like Ancestry) (Labrador and Chilton, 2009).

Studies in the field of 'everyday life information seeking' (Savolainen, 1995) and the 'serious leisure perspective' (Stebbins, 2007) have provided a framework for studying these information-seeking users or heritage amateurs and how they interact with their collections of interest. Skov (2013) found that the information needs of two different groups of what I call heritage amateurs were surprisingly well defined.

On the other hand, I have experienced several heritage professionals who lament the lack of general curation of online collections. Their argument is often that the general public needs curation of the dataset in order to get any use from it.

Thus, there may be a mismatch between the identified uses by heritage amateurs and the perceived uses by the general public. In all circumstances this is an area where we will, hopefully, see much more research in the coming years. Here, the lesson must be the need to explore what the uses of OHD publication can be, not limited to a narrow group of academics or a widely defined 'general public'.

Technical skills

One issue that I believe is exaggerated when it comes to heritage reuse is that of technical skills, whether that the users lack them or that those with technical skills are not interested in heritage. This comes back to a general divide between culture and technology. We see it in our universities and in schools: humanities versus STEM (science, technology, engineering and mathematics), history versus natural science, culture versus digital. I call it exaggerated because making a video for YouTube, sharing stories on Facebook or making GIFs (Graphics Interchange Format) for Instagram does not require very much in terms of technical knowledge. A decade's experience in teaching technical skills and programming to humanities scholars, students and professionals has shown me that it is possible. However, it does require a different approach than that which is perhaps traditionally taught in computer science, an approach that is closer to the ideas of open source concepts. Learning by doing! The coding section in Appendix B and the tutorials in Chapters 5–7 are built on the tutorials I have used to teach students at the University of Copenhagen, Denmark. The idea behind this approach is that anyone can learn to code and use open data if they are motivated and given the right tools to get started. The approach I use is driven by usefulness. Once you have learnt the basic concepts of a new programming language you need to learn only the techniques that are useful to you right now. There is no need to understand the detailed logic of object-oriented programming if all you want to do is present a simple list of items from a dataset. It may seem controversial, but I have seen time and time again how humanities students and scholars can get started with coding as long as the learning curve begins where they are. The first tutorial in the next chapter begins with the very basics of using open data to display a list of poems in a browser. After this you might need a bit more practice to get through some of the tutorials in Chapters 5, 6 and 7, but you will not need a computer science degree.

This does not mean that lack of technical skill or, rather, insecurities and uneasiness about technology is not an issue standing in the way of using open data. A total lack of programming skill and experience can make people believe that working with these datasets is difficult and time consuming, thus making them willing to either pay a great deal of money to developers or to maintain their datasets offline altogether. Lack of technological skills can be a stumbling point, but often it is lack of technological understanding that is holding back heritage professionals and institutions from engaging with open data.

Further, a lack of technological understanding in heritage institutions can result in publications of OHD – for example through an API – with little to no documentation, or with documentation that requires a great amount of pre-knowledge in order to use the resource. When developing an open data resource, such as an API, institutions should prioritise user-friendly documentation and easy-to-use beginners' guides. These are an immense aid, even for the more advanced programmer. This is also a focus point for larger collection providers such as Europeana:

> Due to their different nature, the Europeana Collections and APIs require a different level of user skills. While everyone can search our collections, share, download and reuse the openly licensed records without any previous experience or knowledge, the use of the API would require a rather high level of technical expertise. Of course, our detailed API documentation and dedicated support (Google group and API email address) aim to help the user as much as possible in this task.
>
> (M. Popova, personal communication, 2019)

Making APIs more accessible is thus a focus point for Europeana as well as many other heritage data providers.

Authority

One of the most important and common ways in which heritage is used is through story-telling and outreach. This is often within the confines of more or less official structures like museums, published books, TV or film. These all carry a great authority when it comes to communicating information about heritage – an authority that historically has given them the monopoly on story-telling (Howard, 2003, 247). The internet has somewhat challenged this monopoly in that it has made it easier for other stories to surface. More people can now, potentially, publish their own special-interest heritage collections online and share them with like-minded people across the world. An example of this is the YouTube web series *Ask a Slave* (askaslave.com), which ran for two seasons in 2013 (Dungey and Black, 2013). The series was based on Azie Mira Dungey's experience of working as a historical re-enactor at the Mount Vernon plantation in Virginia, USA. Mount Vernon was the home of the first president of the USA, George Washington, and Martha Dandridge Custis Washington, their family and hundreds of slaves in the 18th century. In the web series, written by Dungey, she plays a fictional slave on the plantation called Lizzie Mae, and she answers questions that are based on real questions she was asked by the public during her time as a re-enactor. The questions range from 'How did you get to be housemaid for such a distinguished founding father?' to 'If you are working all day, who watches your children?' and she answers them with humour and sarcasm in an attempt to point out the continuing racism and sexism in the US of today and to provide information on this aspect of American history from a perspective that is not often heard. The show is not affiliated with the museum or with any other institution usually involved in historical outreach but is, rather, the result of Dungey's work as an actor and writer and her experience. Although it is not based on any dataset it is nevertheless an example of the kind of story-telling and outreach that can come out of private citizens' special interest. OHD can serve as a means to encourage and enable these kinds of endeavours.

In 2011 Terras studied the phenomenon of non-professional content curators using Flickr as a platform for the curation of different heritage collections. The purpose of her paper was to show traditional memory institutions how they can learn from these heritage amateurs when it comes to online collections that are useful, interesting and, most importantly, used by online communities. A few years later many (particularly larger) institutions had taken action and began providing online collections of – especially – their image datasets. In particular, national galleries and art museums saw the value in showing off the parts of their collections not on exhibition, in an online setting.

In comparison, many archives and museums are struggling because they typically have much larger collections of material hidden away, for which the provenance is either unknown or unclear, making it much more difficult to publish online with a clear licence. This means that whereas art museums have an easier time allowing the public to use and reuse their materials through online and open datasets, it is much more difficult for other types of institutions.

Archaeological collections are a good example of this. Most archaeological excavations today produce a huge amount of data (e.g. lists of finds with amounts, sizes and descriptions, masses of images and maps of the excavation and the traces of contexts found). An example is Open Context (see Chapter 3) which provides a platform for publishing archaeological datasets online, and even then only a limited type of data, namely contexts with a small description and a location. However, this is a very small part of the archaeological datasets that are stored in museums, universities and government bodies around the world, and these datasets are growing in number, due to more rigorous digital recording possibilities. Still, any research into archaeological phenomena must be done through published results or access via personal contacts. In other words, potentially enormous amounts of already digital, somewhat structured material that could be used for archaeological research is just not openly available.

Heritage hackathons

Hacking is a cultural phenomenon that could once be found on the fringes of the IT industry and has now become more mainstream. Hacking is all about innovation, play and creativity. It is not, as many might think, about breaking into and stealing things – these people are known in the hacker community as 'crackers'. While the ethos of hacking might be to move fast and break things, it is only in order to make things better, often as a reaction to those who want things to stay the same (Rayner, 2018, 12).

A hackathon is an event, usually over a few days and perhaps nights, where a group of people meet to collaborate on software development. Hackathons often aim to bring together computer programmers with graphic designers, project managers and domain experts. In the case of heritage hackathons, we often find heritage professionals as the domain experts.

I have attended a few of the Danish heritage hackathons (Hack4DK; hack4.dk) over the years, and surveyed a number of participants with different backgrounds in 2015. They were asked to evaluate whether a series of statements were important to them or not, and, while the sample is too small to answer any definitive questions about the participants in Danish heritage hackathons or heritage hackathons in general, there was some agreement among the replies when it came to people's motivation for participating. Most replies agreed that 'Playing with heritage datasets' and having 'A fun and enjoyable weekend' were very important motivations. Following this, many replied that 'Socialising with likeminded people' and 'Contributing my skills to cultural heritage' were also very important motivations. On the other hand, many agreed that showing off skills to private companies, the heritage sector or other hackers was not important. In other words, back in 2015 all of this was new and the heritage data providers were a very small group of people in Denmark, still experimenting with open data, who saw Hack4DK as an opportunity to gauge the potential interest in their datasets among software developers. To my mind the Hack4DK events were a great opportunity to meet with the – unfortunately very small – subsection of heritage professionals with an interest in open data, as well as with the also small group of computer scientists interested in heritage material.

The main motivation behind the Hack4DK events that have been held at different heritage institutions, mainly in the capital, Copenhagen, was to showcase the opportunities that lie in OHD and motivate heritage institutions to go down this route and make more of their digital and digitised datasets available in formats that can be reused. At the time Hack4DK began in 2012 it was a very small group from mainly the largest heritage institutions in Denmark who were working with providing open data. The development of this is still very slow, but moving forward. Heritage institutions in other countries have also hosted a similar type of event. Neighbours to Denmark arrange similar Hack4SE (Sweden), Hack4FI (Finland), Hack4NO (Norway) and a collaborative Hack4Norden in 2016 in Helsinki, Finland which served as a kind of finals for the winners of the Nordic country hackathons. However, while hackathons often serve as a type of competition, it seems that the motivation in heritage hackathons leans more towards socialising and experimenting with heritage datasets.

Heritage hackathons come in many forms and sizes. Because of the size of the countries and the heritage institutions, the hackathons in the Nordic countries are a collaboration between all of a country's institutions with open data. In other parts of the world institutions are larger and are able to host hackathons on their own, an example being the hackathon in 2018 (#hackAN2018) hosted by the Archives Nationales in France (archives-nationales.culture.gouv.fr). Here the national archives hosted a weekend hackathon with eight set challenges based on eight different datasets from the archives (Archives Nationales, 2018).

Other hackathons comprise a theme rather than an institution. An example of this is Hackathon Bandung, a collaboration between the German Goethe-Institut Bandung, the French Institut Français d'Indonesie and the Bandung Heritage Society in Indonesia to host a hackathon focusing on Bandung heritage. The hacks at this event seem to focus mainly on incorporating digital design into the heritage sector. There is no mention of heritage datasets on the website; rather, the 'participants will be working on topics exploring the rich Bandung inner city heritage, both tangible and intangible. They are invited to explore the chosen track and produce an idea. They will be invited to take users' views, feasibility, and business potential into account. Mentors with history, anthropology, architecture, IT backgrounds will help them in developing the idea into a project' (Hackathon Bandung, 2018). In other words, the heritage material they will be given to work with is the heritage experts and their knowledge rather than actual datasets. There can be many reasons for this but a likely issue could be the lack of digital datasets on the heritage in question. Without such datasets, the hackathon takes on a different dimension where the participants must come up with and create their own datasets for the software ideas they are working on.

This begs the question: how do you innovate on heritage and heritage data when it is not openly available? In many countries today, there are digital heritage projects well under way. The heritage sector has been using computer systems since the 1970s (Terras, 2011). But not much of this is available as open data that can be used for cultural innovation. Levy (1984) wrote of the 1950s computers that they were monitored by a priesthood of technicians who were the only people allowed to touch the machines. Anyone wishing to submit data for processing by the machines had to do so through the priesthood. In the same way, today the big data repositories of digitised and born-digital heritage, often built with public funds or volunteer help, are accessible only via a priesthood of technicians in heritage institutions. And in the same way as in the 1950s and onwards, we may find that we will need to hack our way to innovation from the outside in.

Wikipedians

Wikipedia.org is undoubtedly one of the most important heritage resources online (Rosenzweig, 2006). Nevertheless, it embodies the same implicit and explicit bias as most other heritage resources. One solution to this could be to use Wikipedia as a platform for online publishing of heritage material that is not typically exhibited on- or offline by institutions because it is deemed to be too niche (Roued-Cunliffe, 2017). The main stumbling point here is Wikipedia's notability test, where editors can choose to delete articles about subjects that are not deemed notable enough. This is an issue that is currently creating much discussion among Wikipedians and heritage professionals.

The Wikimedia Foundation seems to be very aware of the need to collaborate with heritage institutions in order to bring their resources to Wikipedia. In order to organise this work on a higher plane there is the GLAM-Wiki initiative, which provides a beginners' guide, inspiration and support for GLAM institutions wanting to connect with seasoned Wikipedians to publish their collection and knowledge on a platform that gets millions of page views per day. This is the so-called Wikipedian-in-Residence programme (Wikipedia, 2019b).

The Children's Museum of Indianapolis, USA, has had a Wikipedian in Residence since August 2010. The Wikipedian, Lori Phillips, has facilitated various collaborative projects between the museum and Wikipedia. These include the donation of close to 300 images of collection items to Wikipedia, as well as a QR (Quick Response) code project used around the world and the improvement or creation of articles on museum-related subjects (Wikipedia, 2019c).

Like the Children's Museum of Indianapolis, other heritage institutions have also decided to use Wikipedia as a platform to publish related subjects, especially images. Some, such as the Dutch Rijksmuseum, have uploaded thousands of images that are also available with free culture licences in their own online publication.

> Wikipedia editors prefer to use trusted material provided by the cultural institutions themselves to illustrate the articles they are editing. This greatly benefits both the users who have a richer experience, and the cultural institution that reaches out to a public far beyond the scope of its own website
>
> (Pekel, 2014, 8–9)

While the collaboration between GLAM institutions and Wikipedians is not without its issues, there seems to still be a strong current towards institutions using Wikipedia as a platform for online publication to reach a much wider audience than would be possible by the institution alone. While larger institutions across the world have taken a lead on this work, there are a lot of benefits for smaller institutions too.

Education and youth

OHD is of great use in education settings, as it enables youth to work actively with heritage both via new technologies and through more analogue creative pursuits. For example, this could be through digital mashups and GIFs, dressing up in historical clothing or drawing historic maps of their local area. Many, if not most, heritage institutions understand the value of educational outreach and devote time and resources to this. I have yet to hear of a project that specifically uses APIs to allow young people to develop a dataset. However, there are many projects enabling schoolkids to work with open datasets, sometimes digitally and sometimes physically. One example is from the city of Kolding, Denmark, where the city archive has developed an educational programme allowing local children to use and interact with some of the archive's open datasets.

In their new strategy (2019–22), Kolding City Archives focus on the idea that everyone has a place in history, while recognising that not everyone's history is preserved so that it is available for the future. Especially at risk are private and local materials that will be preserved only if the local community and the archive collaborate on this. Their approach is very democratic and participatory, not only towards the local adult population but also towards the youth and schools in their area. They provide teaching programmes for local education that aim to make sure that all local children have been introduced to the archive at least once during their primary education. Parallel to this, the archive aims to provide open access as well as to support different and creative ways to use their collections (Kolding Stadsarkiv, 2019).

In 2015 the archive began to digitise collections of early portrait photographs and made these images available as open data through Flickr (see Case study 1.5). I have previously written about this open dataset and how to develop sustainable open heritage datasets like it (Roued-Cunliffe, 2018). This dataset is also being used by the archive to engage pupils in reflections on their own and their community's place in history, as well as in working with the images through creative play. Figure 4.1 on the next page shows the pupils creating collages and adding their own artwork to copies of these historic portraits.

Figure 4.1 *Students working with Aagaard's Photos (Kolding City Archives, CC BY)*

Of course, if the students needed to use these images only at the archive they would not need to be accessible as open data. But because they are available as open data any archive, school or private person can replicate this idea and use this material, whether they are in Denmark or anywhere else in the world. Further, children who create something special of their own based on this material are now free to share it however they choose. They can use it to make their own family history documentary or book, as well as to share on social media and websites without having to worry about legal issues.

Apps

In recent years a few apps have been developed based on heritage datasets. Some of these as games, mainly for children, while others are for tourists and visitors to GLAM institutions.

Art Stories Faces (artstories.it/en/faces) is an educational game developed as an app by the Italian start-up Art Stories. The game has been developed with the support of Europeana Labs and uses paintings from the Rijksmuseum in Amsterdam and the Metropolitan Museum in New York that are available as open data. However, it does not seem to use an actual API to access any further data for the app.

The idea behind the game is that children get to play with 30 different paintings, and through this learn the basics of visual art. The player is encouraged to explore different details of the paintings, make jigsaw puzzles and discover secrets. The app won the Europeana Challenge 2016 and has a couple of positive reviews on Google Play. However, as of 2019 it has had only around 500 installations, so it cannot be said to be wildly popular.

During the 2015 Hack4DK (see above) a group of four participants developed the winning project, a game called 'Stamp It'. The idea was that postage stamps fall from the top of the screen and you have to catch them with an envelope, getting an exact amount of postage to pass each level (Lorentzen et al. 2015). The stamps are from a database of Danish stamps (Post & Tele Museum, n.d.), provided by the then Post & Tele Museum (ptt-museum.dk) as a SQL (Structured Query Language) file and a folder of JPG images of each stamp. The database itself can still be found through the Hack4DK dataset documentation for the 2015 event, but the dataset with images is not available as open data as such. As a participant in the 2015 Hack4DK I tried out the prototype of the game and found it to be simple and fun in the same way as other puzzle games. Unfortunately, the team never developed the game any further and the prototype is no longer hosted online.

While some apps are aimed at game-play, others are for tourists wanting to explore a city, area or museum. The Rijksmuseum, Amsterdam has developed such an app (Rijksmuseum, 2019a), which allows their guests to buy tickets, get offers and navigate the museum. You can create your own tour of the museum based on a collection of art you want to visit, which you can create for yourself in the museum's online Rijksstudio system (see Chapter 3).

In a similar vein, the app Vizgu (vizgu.com) allows visitors to point their smartphone camera at a painting in the SMK and view metadata, descriptive texts and sometimes audio on their screens. However, Vizgu is not developed by the SMK, but by a group of Danish developers using the SMK's open data to create this platform. As Jonas Heide Smith, from SMK says, 'We do not want to be app developers, we want to be providers of data, content and knowledge. We want to enable anyone with a good idea to use any portion of our data to enrich their website, app, or service. In this way, we arguably outsource the development and maintenance of SMK-related services freeing us to work on the quality of the data itself' (Smith, 2017).

Greetings from Zagreb (pozdravizhrvatske.nsk.hr/zagrebapp) is an example of an app designed for tourists, allowing them to discover the city of Zagreb, Croatia, through historical postcards and photographs placed on a map. The app was developed by the National and University Library in Zagreb (NSK; nsk.hr) and is powered by the Zagreb Tourist Board (infozagreb.hr). The images used are a part of the NSK's collection and are also available on Europeana. The app also has a 'then and now' feature where you can use a slider to see a new and an old image of a certain part of the town side by side.

Finally, libraries around the world have also developed apps allowing users to access their vast materials through their mobile devices. One such example is the app for the National Digital Library of India (NDL; ndl.iitkgp.ac.in). NDL has integrated content from different institutional repositories and thus acts as a portal allowing everyone to search the material. However, access to full-text materials is usually granted through institutional memberships. Neither the metadata nor the content is necessarily open data.

DIY and maker culture

Reuse of heritage material, especially images of heritage material for custom products and textiles, has boomed in recent years because of new printing technology. If you want to have a T-shirt with the Venus of Willendorf, or a mug with an Emily Dickinson poem, there are many online providers that will let you design your own. However, you need to provide the imagery and it must of course have an open licence (see Chapter 2) or be in the public domain. With the first example this is difficult, as the Natural History Museum Vienna, Austria (nhm-wien.ac.at), where the Venus resides, does not provide images with an open licence. Alternatively, an online search for images of 'Venus of Willendorf' with open licences reveals that both Wikimedia and Flickr host various options.

Printing custom textiles and fabric is a relatively new option for turning your favourite heritage material into items such as clothing and soft furnishings. One of the largest companies providing this is Spoonflower (spoonflower.com), where Quinn Dombrowski printed fabric with the Codex Assemanius, which she then made into a blouse (Figure 4.2). It took

Figure 4.2 *Blouse with Glagolitic text (Quinn Dombrowski, CC BY-SA)*

Dombrowski eight hours to turn eight folios of the Codex into a design that she could then upload to Spoonflower and order as fabric (Dombrowski, 2010). The final image file that she uploaded is also available on Flickr with an open licence and anyone can order fabric or wallpaper with this design, or with other designs made by Dombrowski from medieval Slavic material.

The Rijksmuseum in Amsterdam has hosted the Rijksstudio award a couple of times, the first award being given in 2014 and the latest to be given in 2020. The 'Make your own Masterpiece' competition invited participants to be inspired by the museum's collection and create their own designs using the Rijksstudio platform. The winners' and finalists' projects range from a knitting pattern for a hat inspired by Delft Blue Porcelain to sleep masks with eyes from famous paintings on the front (Rijksmuseum, 2019b).

Portals

In 2007 I wrote my master's thesis on the subject 'Heritage Portals and Cross-border Data Interoperability'. One of my points was that the potential of web service technology (now generally known as APIs) could encourage data sharing in the international heritage sector, as well as enabling the development of heritage portals such as the later Europeana portal. APIs as we know them today certainly can and have enabled this, but, I would argue, not to the extent that I hoped back in 2007. For this project I mapped two datasets to each other (see tutorials of how to do this in Chapter 6) and presented the two datasets in a combined search. One of the datasets was of my own making and based on data I had painstakingly collected through published sources for my bachelor's dissertation (Roued Olsen, 2007b) on finds that connected South Scandinavia and the Sîntana de Mures/Çernjachov cultures in present-day Ukraine and Romania during the Late Roman Iron Age period (270–410 CE). The other dataset was from the Swedish National Heritage Board, with archaeological find sites (the map tutorial in Chapter 6 uses their current open data). I was able to find enough similarities in the two datasets that when I searched for something like 'axe' I got a result of find sites with axes from both sources. I then used the geographical locations to create a map of the combined results.

Portals such as Europeana (see Chapter 3 for a further exploration of this), which combines metadata for heritage items from across Europe, do so by pulling data from institutional APIs as well as by manual export/import of datasets. Most often this publication of metadata to the Europeana portal happens through aggregators on a national, domain or thematic level. To date, Europeana has collected the metadata of nearly 60 million heritage items from across Europe. This seems like a lot, but in reality, it is a very small amount of the combined heritage data of Europe. Even so, it is increasingly important for Europeana to curate and provide outreach for this dataset. Even though it contains only metadata it is a great resource, but also surprisingly under-used in the larger context of things. In my experience, not many people outside of heritage professionals know about Europeana, and even among heritage professionals only a few use it.

This could be seen as a lack of interest in heritage and heritage portals or OHD. But I do not think that is the case. Rather, I believe that Europeana as an institution, just like all other heritage institutions, has difficulty reaching out to other than a small, special interest group. This is the real power of open data. Europeana Collections as a search platform of 60 million more or less random heritage items from across Europe is not in itself valuable to the wider public. Rather, the potential applications, tools and new projects that can come out of Europeana as an open data provider are valuable to a wider population.

Let us first look at a portal developed outside of these institutions but using their APIs. The Culture Collage (zenlan.com/collage) pulls images from the following institutions' API's: Europeana, Digital Public Library of America, Trove National Library of Australia, Digital New Zealand, Imperial War Museums, Royal Museums Greenwich, Victoria & Albert Museum, Science Museum Group, Wellcome Collection, Flickr Commons, the British Library and the Internet Archive, and displays them in different ways depending on the search. The portal is developed by Monique Szpak at Zenlan and is not, as such, associated with any of the institutions that it uses, apart from the fact that Szpak has worked as a developer for some of them and so she has some inside knowledge. This confirms the point made above, that these collections in themselves do not have an immediate public interest or use; rather, they are often used by people with connections to the heritage field – perhaps developers who want to show their skills and get jobs with the institutions in question, or students and researchers across the world and heritage data geeks doing it for the fun of it.

Monique says of the portal:

> I was participating in a remote hackathon for International Women's Day and posted a link to a search of the V&A collections for 'women'. The search results were quite stunning and to my surprise the link (www.zenlan.com/collage/vam/#women) was retweeted and gained quite a bit of interest. I realised that it might be worth working on my bit of training code, that people other than myself might find it fun/useful. It became my side-project and I used it to update my technical skills and as a bit of a showcase/skills demo. Unlike many of my previous training projects, Culture Collage was something I actually used and enjoyed.
>
> (M. Szpak, personal communication, 2019)

Another portal for browsing heritage images is the On This Day project (culturepics.org/on-this-day) developed by James Morley, who has harvested data sources for specific dates from the following heritage APIs: Europeana, Archives de la Planète, Open Data Hautes-de-Seines, Imperial War Museums, Lives of the First World War, National Maritime Museum, Flickr Commons, American Air Museum. The code that James has built is also licensed as open source, meaning that it is available to copy, modify and distribute freely. This portal is dependent on the metadata from the different datasets, including dates as well as images.

Tools

Another way that APIs are often used is to create new tools to explore the collections. Figure 4.3 shows an example of the visually exciting Europeana Colour Explorer (culturepics.org/colour) built by James Morley to showcase new metadata added to the Europeana API in 2015 (Europeana, 2016). It is an interesting way to explore images in Europeana based on their colour tone and it demonstrates a tool developed in a playful spirit to enable a different, fun way to interact with the dataset.

Another tool option is simply to call an API for items on a particular subject and display a list of these objects. The first tutorial in the Chapter 5 section 'Basic data reuse' shows how to do this. It has been done for the National Library of Australia (Trove) API, for which there is a tool which lists all knitting patterns

Figure 4.3 *Screenshot of Europeana Colour Explorer (culturepics.org/colour) by James Morley, with the colour 'black', using data from the Europeana API*

in Trove (Trove, 2019b), with a link to the original pattern text, the publication, the date and a link to share each pattern on Twitter – an example of a very simple tool developed for a very specific purpose or smaller user group. OHD makes it possible to develop these kinds of tools for specific user groups.

The Spanish software company DIGIBÍS (digibis.com) specialises in digital solutions for heritage institutions and in this vein has developed a tool for comparing the results of a search in DPLA and Europeana. The result is a simple list (25 items at a time) of items from each source, containing images, metadata and links back to the source as well as a comparison of the full amount of results. Chapter 6 will include tutorials on combining datasets from different API sources in a similar way.

MovesScrapbook is a tool developed within the Culture Moves project (culturemoves.eu) in order to encourage reuse of Europeana content for touristic engagement and educational purposes. The idea is that anyone can sign up for an account and create their own scrapbooks by mixing Europeana content with their own material in order to create stories to share with teachers or on social media.

QueryPic (dhistory.org/querypic) is another type of tool, created by Tim Sherratt, which enables the exploration of trends and patterns in digital newspapers from the Australian Trove and New Zealand's Papers Past. The tool visualises a simple search in one of the two databases as a line plotted over time. Once a plot has been created it can be saved and shared with other users. For example, one plot shows the connection between the two terms 'beauty' and 'youthfulness', created by user 'Jamie' on 20 October 2019. This visualisation shows a peak in newspaper articles that link these two terms between the 1830s and the 1880s. While this is a nifty and interesting tool, Chapter 7 will explore the validity of these results. Nevertheless, tools like this make heritage datasets more widely available for a wider audience.

Summary

This chapter has:

1 discussed different issues in relation to the reuse of openly published heritage data, including that of the users themselves as well as technical skills and who has the authority to mediate heritage;
2 illustrated how groups of heritage hackers and Wikipedians collaborate with heritage institutions in order to mediate heritage to new audiences;
3 illustrated with examples how heritage data can be reused for educational purposes, games and guide apps, as well as in DIY and maker culture;

4 exemplified how open heritage datasets are used for cross-search portals as well as various specialised tools.

## 5

Visualising open data

I will admit that datasets are often complicated and rather boring to look at unless you are able to see the beauty behind the labels and fields. Take, for example, this snippet of GeoJSON from a dataset of street trees in Copenhagen that can be found on the Open Data DK platform (opendata.dk).

```
[...],{"type":"Feature","id":"gadetraer.2","geometry":{"type":"Point",
"coordinates":[12.582691256406196,55.69229362391806]},"geometry_name":
"wkb_geometry","properties":{"id":14313,"traeart":"Tilia europaea",
"slaegt":"Tilia sp.","dansk_navn":"Park-Lind","slaegtsnavn":"Lind",
"planteaar":"1960",[...]}},[...]
```

To most people this snippet of code looks very confusing (not only because of the mix of Danish and English) and is something that would not have much value in itself. But if you are able to look behind the commas and curly brackets you will see a vast amount of really interesting information (if trees and gardening are your thing, of course!). It tells us that for one specific tree we have the coordinates in longitude and latitude. This allows us to plot the tree as a point on a map. We can see that the tree in question is a Tilia europaea, the Latin name for a common lime tree, and that it was planted in 1960. This information can be used to determine which icon to place on the map, like in Figure 5.1 on the next page.

We could also use the information for labels, or use the date to overlay the icons with different depth of colour so that younger trees appear lighter than older ones.

Another way of visualising this particular dataset could be as a list of tree types with the quantity of each, as shown here:

- Ambratræ, Liquidambar sp. (25 / 0.13%)
- Ask, Fraxinus sp. (1398 / 7.39%)
- Avnbøg, Carpinus sp. (179 / 0.95%)
- Birk, Betula sp. (267 / 1.41%)
- Bærmispel, Amelanchier sp. (27 / 0.14%).

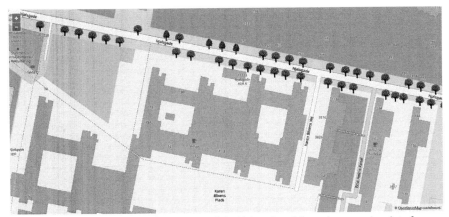

Figure 5.1 *Map visualisation of trees around the University of Copenhagen, using data from Copenhagen Municipality (opendata.dk), CC BY*

A third option could be to visualise this sorted and counted dataset as a bar chart with tree types along the y-axis and percentages along the x-axis (Figure 5.2).

All in all, having access to raw data is a powerful thing that enables us to visualise and combine datasets in new and interesting ways.

Previous chapters have shown examples of publishing and reusing heritage data with varying degrees of openness. However, this chapter and the following two chapters will deal with heritage data that is made available as

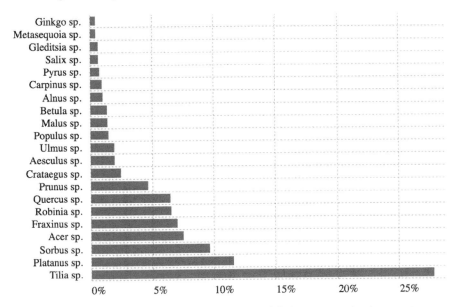

Figure 5.2 *Bar chart of tree families in Copenhagen and their representation in percentages, using data from Copenhagen Municipality (opendata.dk), CC BY*

raw data through APIs, according to the fifth and final question in the OHD Model.

This chapter will demonstrate how to visualise different heritage datasets in a basic way as lists, images, maps and charts. Chapter 6 will combine two or more different datasets in order to visualise these in new ways. Chapter 7 will show examples of how to clean and analyse these datasets.

The following tutorials require a very basic knowledge of HTML, CSS, PHP, JavaScript, and Python. If you have no pre-existing knowledge of these coding languages I would suggest having a look at the coding introductions in Appendix B.

Basic data reuse

In this first tutorial I will demonstrate how to pull data from a heritage API and use this to create a basic list. I have chosen to pull data from PoetryDB (poetrydb.org), which is an open source/open data initiative that publishes (currently only) English language poems in the public domain. As far as I can see, the project is not affiliated with any institution and it is unclear who built the database. This is of course something to take into consideration when deciding to use a dataset from the web. Not every dataset is published legally, and not every dataset creator cares about issues such as copyright and data protection (see Chapter 2 for more on this). In this case, however, I will use poems by the author Emily Brontë, who died in 1848 and whose work is in the public domain.

Step 1

The first step when calling up an API to retrieve data is to create the URL that combines the parameters you want to send to the API (see Chapter 1 for more on APIs and URL requests). Each API has a root URL, which in this case is 'http://poetrydb.org'. Most APIs also have different methods that can be used to access the dataset. For example, there might be a *search* method allowing you to search through the dataset with a query, or there might be a record method, allowing you to access a particular record if you know the record ID, which you will often find through the search method. In this way API methods are often interconnected.

For PoetryDB there are four methods allowing us to search through the four different elements of the dataset: author, title, lines and line count. For this search we will use the method *author* to find the poems in the dataset by the author Emily Brontë. The URL looks like this:

```
http://poetrydb.org/author/Emily%20Bronte
```

The sign '%20' is URL code for a space (e.g. between Emily and Bronte). This is because a blank space is not allowed in a URL. Also, the 'ë' at the end is changed to a plain 'e' to include it in the URL, as only Latin characters A–z (i.e. the English language alphabet) are allowed, along with numbers 0–9 and certain other symbol characters. Any other character must be encoded.

Encoding can be necessary when working with heritage data, as many languages include different symbols than those included in the English language. Danish is one such language with its three extra vowels: æ, ø and å, and other languages also have this. Some languages use different scripts, such as Cyrillic, which is used in the national languages of many East European countries, or logogram writing systems, such as Chinese and some Egyptian hieroglyphs.

Step 2

The next step is to copy the URL into a browser to check that you are getting a result and not an error message. This result may look very messy, depending on the API. Instead you can copy the URL into a JSON or XML code beautifier (you can find various tools like this through a quick online search).

This will provide you with an overview of the returned code and show you the paths to the elements you need. It makes it easier to search and find elements you might need to extract for your code. In this case the dataset is rather simply formatted, even without a code beautifier, but in many cases the API result is very chaotic and/or complex. Using the 'search' function, you will also be able to see if each record has a specific element. For example, in this case the call returns 14 records of Emily Brontë poems and a search for 'author' also gives 14 results, telling me that each record has an 'author' element. However, a search for the number '32' gives three results and tells me that only three of the records have a line count of 32.

Step 3

Now for some coding. In this simple example we will publish a very basic list of the titles for Emile Brontë's poems. This code uses PHP and a little HTML. The code below does the following.

1   It specifies the API URL in a variable ($api_URL).
2   It imports the file content into a different variable ($json_file).
3   It decodes the JSON file into a variable ($resource_array).

4 The variable ($resource_array) is then looped (using foreach) and each record is output temporarily into the variable $value.
5 In the loop the title for each record is printed (using echo). Through the beautifier we can see that the path to the 'title' element in each numbered record is simply '-> title'.
6 In the loop the HTML code for a horizontal line '<hr/>'is printed for each record.
7 Finally, the loop is closed and so is the PHP code.

```php
<?php
// PoetryDB
// specify the API URL
$api_URL = 'http://poetrydb.org/author/Emily%20Bronte';
// get content from the JSON file
$json_file = file_get_contents($api_URL);
// decode JSON file into a variable
$resource_array = json_decode($json_file);
// loop through each record
foreach ($resource_array as $value){
  // print title
  echo $value->title;
  // print horizontal line
  echo "<hr/>";
} // loop end
?>
```

Result

Figure 5.3 on the next page shows that the result is a very simple list of titles with a horizontal line below each title. This list can be styled in different ways: instead of horizontal lines I could have used the HTML elements for a numbered list (i.e. <ol> and <li>) or I could have added the list to different existing website designs. The possibilities are many, but this tutorial has shown the simple principle of calling up the API and publishing the data it contains on a web page.

Try it yourself

1 Try to extract the titles for another poet from poetrydb.org.
2 Try to print the titles as a numbered list.
3 Try to extract and print the titles with the term 'spring' as an unnumbered list.

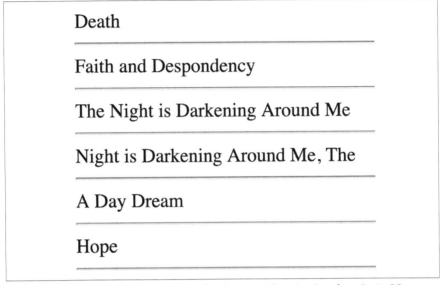

Death

Faith and Despondency

The Night is Darkening Around Me

Night is Darkening Around Me, The

A Day Dream

Hope

Figure 5.3 *The result of the code: a print of each poem title, using data from PoetryDB (poetrydb.org), CC BY*

Images

The previous tutorial demonstrated how to pull data from a heritage API and use it to create a simple list. Now you will learn how to extract data from an API and display images. In this example we will use Museums Victoria Collections (collections.museumvictoria.com.au), which is an Australian repository of over 17 million items of environmental and cultural history. The museums include collections in geology, historical studies, indigenous cultures, palaeontology, technology and science and zoology. The metadata is licensed under Creative Commons Zero (CC0) and the text is licensed under Creative Commons Attribution 4.0 International (CC-BY). Images on the site are licensed individually, with a substantial part marked as Public domain. However, not every item has an image. Therefore, for the purposes of this tutorial we will specify in our API URL that we want to retrieve only items with images.

A link to the API is displayed very prominently on the collection's website in the main menu, making it visible for everyone, not just internal staff or external developers. The documentation provides many examples, which makes it easy to get started with the API.

Step 1
We will call the following URL:

```
https://collections.museumvictoria.com.au/api/search?query=flowers&hasimages
=yes&sort=relevance&perpage=100&imagelicence=public+domain
```

This URL consists of the main API URL (https://collections.museumvictoria.com.au/api), the method (/search?), the search term (query=flowers), the parameter specifying that we want records with images only (hasimages=yes), the sorting parameter (sort=relevance) and finally the number of records per result call (perpage=100). The default records per call is 40 and the maximum is 100, with the option to paginate. Pagination in this context means that the API provider returns a set number of items (e.g. the first 100), instead of the full list of results. It is then possible to request the next 100 items by requesting page 2 of the same search, in this case by adding '&page=2' to the URL string.

Step 2

The data returned from the call above is long and complex, with 118 elements for each of the 100 records. Through a JSON beautifier we can search for the URLs that we need to display the images in HTML. In this case it takes some trial and error to find these URLs, as they are placed under the path 0->media->0->small>uri.

Step 3

```php
<?php
// Images from Museums Victoria - Australia
// specify the API URL
$api_URL =
'https://collections.museumvictoria.com.au/api/search?query=flowers&hasimage
s=yes&sort=relevance&perpage=100&imagelicence=public+domain';
// get content from the JSON file
$json_file = file_get_contents($api_URL);
// decode JSON file into a variable
$resource_array = json_decode($json_file);
// loop through each record
foreach ($resource_array as $value){
  // get the image URL
  $img = $value->media[0]->small->uri;
  // print image to 200px width
  echo ' <img width="200px" src="', $img, '"/>';
} // loop end
?>
```

The PHP and HTML code above does the following.

1   It specifies the API URL in a variable ($api_URL).
2   It imports the file content into a different variable ($json_file).
3   It decodes the JSON file into a variable ($resource_array).
4   The variable ($resource_array) is then looped (using foreach) and each record is output temporarily into the variable $value.

5 In the loop, the image URL for each record is added to a temporary variable ($img).
6 In the loop, an HTML tag for image display is printed (using echo) with a 200px width and with the image URL.
7 Finally, the loop is closed and so is the PHP code.

Result

Each of the images from the API call is shown in the browser with a width of 200px and varying height, one after the other across the screen. The number of images in each line is dependent on the width of the screen in pixels (Figure 5.4).

Figure 5.4 *The result of the code, with the images from the Museums Victoria Collections (collections.museumvictoria.com.au) displayed side by side, CC BY*

Try it yourself

1 Try a different search term.
2 Try to display the images in a different style, using HTML and CSS.
3 Try to display images with a different licence or without a licence.

Maps

Visualising datasets on maps requires a base map on which to overlay your geographical data layers. It also requires datasets with geographical coordinates. There are several options for base maps. One popular option is Google Maps, which has comprehensive documentation. However, in the spirit of open, we will use the Open Layers (OL) coding library, which includes Open Street Map (OSM) as a base layer. The OSM (openstreetmap.org) project is a collaborative project launched in 2004 in the UK as a response to tax-funded government mapping projects that were acting as for-profit companies in terms of sharing their digital mapping services. The OSM maps are open data and are licensed under the Open Database License, while the cartography (i.e. the map tiles) is licensed as Creative Commons Attribution-ShareAlike 2.0 (CC BY-SA). Any use of the maps must carry an attribution to OSM contributors, a group consisting of thousands of individuals across the world as well as many government bodies donating maps and datasets to the project or giving their data an open licence, enabling OSM to include it.

In this tutorial we will use HTML and the coding language JavaScript (see Appendix B) to retrieve the map from OL and display our open data on this map.

Step 1

For the first step we need to retrieve the data we want to visualise through a URL. In this case however, we retrieve the full dataset from a government open data portal, in this example the Irish government's open data portal, data.gov.ie. This portal lists open data published by government departments and public bodies in Ireland. I searched in this portal for 'heritage' datasets which have an API and use the GeoJSON format. As of writing there were 30 results and I chose to use the dataset on Heritage Walk Stops published by South Dublin County Council (South Dublin County Council, 2018). This dataset consists of 150 records (i.e. stops) divided into nine different routes. Each record has a name for the stop and a link to the route page on the Heritage Walks website.

It seems that this dataset was used to develop audio walks for a mobile app. Through the Internet Archive Wayback Machine, we can see that the website for the South Dublin Heritage Walks (heritagewalks.sdcc.ie) was active between 2013 and 2018. The dataset was uploaded or updated in the Irish open data portal in 2018, perhaps in an attempt to preserve it or to enable others to continue working on it. In any case, it is licensed under a CC BY license, meaning that anyone is free to share and adapt it, even commercially, as long as they attribute South Dublin County Council.

The URL for the GeoJSON version of the dataset is published in the portal to copy into our code and is as follows:

```
http://data-sdublincoco.opendata.arcgis.com/datasets/
173b4ebb3bb442ce8cad018ab48cd12a_1.geojson
```

This time the data that we will use is static, meaning that this is not a link to the live version of the dataset. The dataset will not change and, in theory, we could just download it and use it locally. However, since most people do not have easy access to internet hosting it is important to have open data portals like this from which we can use the data through the URL they provide.

Step 2

As in the previous examples we can view the dataset in a JSON beautifier, but this time there is not much need for this. Earlier we have dealt with datasets that were structured according to standards determined by the provider. However, this time we are using GeoJSON, which is a type of JSON that is designed for encoding geographical data structures along with their non-geographical attributes. The structure of the JSON data is thus always the same and we do not need to identify the paths we need for our map visualisation.

Step 3

The following are the steps in the HTML and JavaScript code.

1 In the HTML head we link to the OL CSS style as well as writing our own CSS style to specify how high and wide we want our map.
2 It links to the OL code library so that we can use their commands (beginning with ol.).
3 In the HTML body we add a div tag with the id 'map'; this is the same tag that we styled above.
4 The next part is written in JavaScript code, where we first create a variable called 'map' to hold the map data.
5 The map consists of two layers, the first being the map from OSM.
6 On top of this layer is our data from the heritage walks. This is where we input the URL from the open data portal.
7 We then style this second layer so that the points are circles with a green fill and a blue edge.
8 We make a viewport for this map centred on the coordinates for South Dublin (-6.400000, 53.320000) and with the spatial reference set to WGS (World Geodetic System) 84 (EPSG:4326) and WGS 84 Web Mercator (EPSG:3857).
9 Finally, we set the beginning zoom of the map to 12. The higher the zoom number, the closer the map will zoom in to begin with.

```html
<html>
  <head>
    <!- HTML comment: Link to openlayers CSS style ->
    <link rel="stylesheet"
href="https://cdn.rawgit.com/openlayers/openlayers.github.io/master/en/
v5.3.0/css/ol.css" type="text/css">
    <style>
      /* CSS comments - style the div container with the id=map */
        #map {
          height: 500px;
          width: 100%;
        }
    </style>
    <!- link to openlayers code library ->
    <script
src="https://cdn.rawgit.com/openlayers/openlayers.github.io/master/en/
v5.3.0/build/ol.js"></script>
  </head>
  <body>
    <!- div container for the map ->
    <div id="map" ></div>
    <!- JavaScript creating the map ->
    <script type="text/javascript">
      // JavaScript comment: create a new map in the variable "map"
      var map = new ol.Map({
        // place the map in the div container with the id = map
        target: 'map',
        // create layers:
        layers: [
          // add the Open Street Map (OSM) as the first layer
          new ol.layer.Tile({
            source: new ol.source.OSM()
          }),
        // add the GeoJSON file from the open data portal as the second
layer
        new ol.layer.Vector({
        // create a new vector source in GeoJSON format using the URL for
the GeoJSON file
        source: new ol.source.Vector({
            format: new ol.format.GeoJSON(),
            // GeoJSON URL
            URL: 'http://data-
sdublincoco.opendata.arcgis.com/datasets/173b4ebb3bb442ce8cad018ab48cd12a_
1.geojson'
        }),
            // style the second layer
        style: new ol.style.Style({
        // style each point as a circle
            image: new ol.style.Circle({
              radius: 8,
              fill: new ol.style.Fill({
                color: 'green'
              }),
```

```
              // style the circle edge
              stroke: new ol.style.Stroke({
                color: 'blue',
                width: 1
              })
            })
          })
        })],
    // set the viewport of the map
      view: new ol.View({
        //center on the coordinates
          center: ol.proj.transform([-6.400000, 53.320000], 'EPSG:4326',
'EPSG:3857'),
          // set the map zoom
          zoom: 12
      })
});
    </script>
  </body>
</html>
```

Result

Figure 5.5 shows the result as OSM base layer of Dublin, with the points from the dataset as green circles with a blue edge.

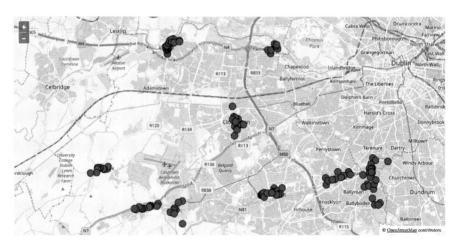

Figure 5.5 *The result of the code: a map of the Heritage Walks published by South Dublin County Council on data.gov.ie, CC BY*

Try it yourself

1 Try a different style for the points on the map.
2 Try using different start coordinates and a different start zoom.
3 Try to find a different GeoJSON dataset on data.gov.ie to display on the map.

Charts

Another popular method for visualising datasets is through charts or graphs. Some datasets lend themselves more toward this than others. Datasets with clear numerical data, such as the quantity, size or weight of archaeological finds, would be very well illustrated on a chart, where we can clearly spot tendencies or explore details in the dataset. Other datasets can be charted only if categories are counted first. For example, counting all the pieces of art created in a certain year or decade, or displaying the gender division of art acquired by a museum over the years.

For this purpose, I will use the open source JavaScript library chartist.js to visualise the dataset onto a chart. Like OSM, chartist.js was also created by developers who were unhappy with the alternatives available at the time. In this example I will call on The National Archives, UK, which has made metadata for more than 32 million records from their own and 2500 other institutions available through their Discovery portal. Discovery enables an API search of these records with a JSON output.

Step 1

This example will search the Discovery portal for records with the phrase 'victory garden' in the metadata. From the Discovery search I know that the result is only 78 records, therefore I have set the cap for results (resultsPageSize) to 100. The default is 15 and the max is 1000, which is quite a high number. The search query is 'victory garden' (%22 is URL code for a quotation mark and %20 is URL code for a space).

```
https://discovery.nationalarchives.gov.uk/API/search/records?sps.searchQuery
=%22victory%20garden%22&sps.resultsPageSize=100
```

Step 2

This results in a JSON dataset with 78 records. For the chart I want to visualise the year and the percentage of the overall records for each year. Many records in Discovery have a start and an end date. In the JSON records we get this both as an actual date and as a number formatted as year, month, date: YYYYMMDD. In this example I am interested in the records' start year, which can be found through the following path: records ->0->numStartDate. The code in step 3 will calculate the percentage of records for each year and create a dataset on the fly (Table 5.1).

Table 5.1 *Table showing the number of records at the start of each year and the calculated percentages*

Year	Number	Percentage
1941	2	2.56%
1942	1	1.28%
1943	13	16.67%
1944	9	11.54%
1945	10	12.82%
1946	6	7.69%
1947	13	16.67%
1952	1	1.28%
1961	3	3.85%
1962	2	2.56%
No date	18	23.08%
Total	78	100%

Step 3

The PHP, JavaScript and HTML code below does the following.

1   It calls and loops the records as in the basic example above.
2   It counts the records and adds this to the $count variable.
3   For each record the 'numStartDate' is retrieved and the first 4 digits (i.e. the year) are added to the $year variable using the substr() function.
4   If the year is not zero, then it adds the year to the array $year_array.
5   Each time the same year occurs in the loop +1 is added to the quantity and the percentage of year occurrences is calculated with the $count variable from before.
6   The year array is sorted in ascending order.
7   In the HTML head the Chartist code library and stylesheet are called.
8   In the HTML body a div is created with the class 'ct-chart' and 'ct-major-twelfth'. The latter is one of several predefined Chartist aspect ratios to choose between.

9   In the JavaScript the data for the labels (x-axis) and series (y-axis) is pulled from the PHP $year_array using a PHP foreach loop.

10 The option settings specify that the y-axis must use whole numbers with a percentage sign after.

11 The Chartist.Bar() function is called, adding the data and options to the div with the class 'ct-chart'.

```php
<?php
// API URL
$api_URL =
'https://discovery.nationalarchives.gov.uk/API/search/records?sps.
searchQuery=%22victory%20garden%22&sps.resultsPageSize=100';
// call the JSON file
$json_file = file_get_contents($api_URL);
// decode JSON file into a PHP array
$resource_array = json_decode($json_file);
// count records and add to $count variable
$count= count($resource_array->records);
// loop through each record
foreach ($resource_array->records as $value){
  // get the date
  $date = $value->numStartDate;
  // get the year from the first 4 digits
  $year = substr($date, 0, 4);
  // place the year in an array if it is not 0
  if ($year != 0){
    $year_array[$year]['year'] = $year;
    // add +1 to the count of each year when it occurs
    $year_array[$year]['amount'] += 1;
    // calculate the percentage of each year in the records
    $year_array[$year]['percentage'] =
round($year_array[$year]['amount']/$count*100, 2);
  }
} // loop end
// sort the years in ascending order
asort($year_array);
// end of php
?>

<!DOCTYPE html>
<html>
  <head>
  <!- links to Chartist code library and stylesheet ->
    <link rel="stylesheet"
href="//cdn.jsdelivr.net/chartist.js/latest/chartist.min.css">
    <script
src="//cdn.jsdelivr.net/chartist.js/latest/chartist.min.js"></script>
  </head>
  <body>
    <!- add div to hold the chart, using predefined Chartist classes->
    <div class="ct-chart ct-major-twelfth"></div>
```

```
<script type="text/javascript">
// start of JS script
// chart build - gather the data
var data = {
// create labels (x-axis)
  labels: [
<?php
// in PHP build a comma separated list of years from the $years_array
foreach ($year_array as $value){
  echo "'" . $value['year'] . "',";}
?> // end of php
  ],
  // create series (y-axis)
  series: [[
<?php
// in PHP build a comma separated list of % from the $years_array
foreach ($year_array as $value){
  echo "" . $value['percentage'] . ",";}
?> // end of php
  ]]
};

var options = {
  // options for the y-axis
  axisY: {
    // no decimal numbers
    onlyInteger: true,
    labelInterpolationFnc: function(value) {
      // add percentage sign to the numbers
      return value + '%';
    }
  }
};
// create the chart in the div with the ct-chart class, using the data and
the options above
new Chartist.Bar('.ct-chart', data, options);
// end of  JS script
</script>
</body>
</html>
```

Result

The result of the code above is a bar chart (Figure 5.6 opposite) with each year in the dataset on the x-axis and the percentage values at the start of each year on the y-axis. This shows that the UK National Archives has records with the mention of 'victory garden' in their collection, beginning from 1941 and with an increase from 1943 to 1947.

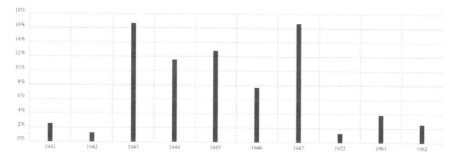

Figure 5.6 *A bar chart of records in the UK National Archives (nationalarchives.gov.uk) containing the phrase 'victory garden' and showing the percentage for each year, CC BY*

Try it yourself

1   Try to search for other records using a different search term.
2   Try making a line chart using the chartist.js documentation.
3   Try charting a different metadata element from the dataset.

Summary

This chapter has:

1   illustrated how to call an API via a URL with certain parameters. The basic reuse tutorial accesses data from the PoetryDB project using the method 'author' and the search term 'Emily Bronte'. The API returns information about Emily Brontë's poems such as the title, the number of lines and the text itself in the JSON format. The PHP code displays the titles as a list by using a PHP loop execution;

2   illustrated how to retrieve image files (or, rather, the URL for image files) from the Museums Victoria Collection, Australia. This requires a specification in the URL for images and for more records than are the default. The PHP code displays the image URLs as a part of an HTML image tag so that the images themselves are displayed side by side in the browser;

3   illustrated how to access a dataset of geographical locations in a geoJSON format of Heritage Walk Stops published by South Dublin County Council, Ireland. Here the whole dataset can be accessed through a single URL retrieved from the Irish Government's Open Data portal. The HTML and JavaScript code displays the points from the dataset on an OSM using the OL code library;

4   illustrated how to access metadata from the Discovery portal of The National Archives, UK. The PHP, JavaScript and HTML code calls the

URL and analyses the metadata returned. It creates a new dataset in a PHP array for the start year of the records returned and the percentage of records from each year. This data is displayed as a chart using the chartist.js code library.

## 6

Combining open data

Combining or mapping datasets serves a very important purpose in terms of open data. This is because the real beauty of open data lies in the ability to use data from different sources together. For example, by creating a simple portal allowing different datasets to be searched and browsed in the same platform – such as the DPLA/Europeana tool shown in Chapter 4, which sends a similar call to both DPLA and Europeana and allows the results to be visualised side by side.

Over the years there have been many attempts to make coherent standards and thesauri for various domains in the heritage sector. As with data sharing, libraries were the prime movers on common data standards, with standards like MARC developed by Henriette Avram in the 1960s for the US Library of Congress (Schudel, 2006). The MARC standards were developed to catalogue library metadata from books, articles and other publications. In the heritage sector books and artworks are some of the easiest items for which to create a common standard, as they often have very similar metadata (e.g. author/ artist, title, publisher, length/size, type/technique/media/genre). However, the need for shared metadata is greater for books than for artworks because there are often many copies of a book in many different institutions which can make use of the shared information. This is why libraries for many years led the drive to share metadata and were able to successfully roll out a metadata standard that most countries use in one form or another.

The current push in sharing metadata for heritage items is driven by galleries and art museums. Many of these heritage data-sharing sites are image based. Images, whether reproductions of artworks or digitisations of documents or photographs, also have a pretty similar metadata structure: creator, date, subject, etc. The use and reuse of the images is heavily reliant on their copyright status, but makes for very interesting projects in creative communities. However, there are large amounts of heritage material that are not so easy to share or to find a data standard for, despite many years of trying. This is because the metadata for these datasets, unlike the metadata for images or books, is not in wide use. For example, the metadata for a table of archaeological finds might tell us who compiled it, which excavation it was from, when it was made and how many items it contains. This information is important, but not interesting to share as open data, as it has limited reuse value, whereas the finds table in itself, with the quantity of finds of different types, their size and find locations, could be very valuable. The issue here is that archaeological excavations around the world do not have a common data standard for how to store these vast amounts of data. I believe that this is because the ways in which these datasets are stored are very closely related to the methodology of the excavation, which, it is my experience, can vary a lot from culture to culture. Another reason why a common data standard is difficult to implement both within archaeology and for other museum items is that data sharing is not a necessity. A library is a pretty useless institution today if users cannot look up which books it has or where they are, whereas a museum will function perfectly well with an informative exhibition out front and a limited overview of what is in the boxes in storage. Archives are another subject, as in some places they are run as libraries or are even a part of libraries, whereas in other places they are their own entities or are connected to museums. Whether they are run by archivists, librarians or historians makes a big difference in the attitude towards their material, datasets and standards.

In the following, I am going to introduce some different records and show how these can be combined, despite the lack of common metadata standards.

The code in the following sections uses PHP, HTML, JSON and CSS – for an introduction to these please refer to the coding section in Appendix B. I would also recommend that beginners work through Chapter 5 before attempting the following tutorials.

Combining art

Open data from galleries or art museums in many instances includes images of art pieces, allowing these datasets to appeal as visually creative projects as well as research and heritage projects. Perhaps this is why galleries across the world have been so quick to jump on this open data bandwagon. As discussed before, artworks, like books, have fairly simple datasets with uncomplicated metadata. In the following example I will demonstrate how we can combine the results from several galleries into one single view.

The first step is to access the datasets through appropriate searches. In this example I will use data from three APIs and combine them into one view. The three datasets are the Dutch Rijksmuseum API (rijksmuseum.nl/en/api), the Finnish National Art Gallery API (kokoelmat.fng.fi/api) and American Harvard Art Museum API (harvardartmuseums.org/collections/api).

Step 1

The first step is to examine each API and test it for a chosen query. In this case we are going to retrieve images of artwork related to botany.

The Dutch Rijksmuseum API requires that you sign up for an account with their user-curator platform, Rijksstudio, in order to apply for an API key (swap the XXXX in the code for your own key). This API can deliver both JSON and XML and gives access to collections, Rijksstudio user-curated sets, an events calendar and more.

```
https://www.rijksmuseum.nl/api/en/collection?format=json&q=garden&imgonly=
true&ps=20&key=XXXX
```

The API request is searching in the collections for the first 20 images of artwork with 'garden' in any of the metadata fields, formatted with JSON.

For the Harvard Art Museum's API we also need to request an API key (swap the YYYY in the code for your own key) because the museum would like to be able to track the users of the API. Despite searching for results with images only, some of the objects do not have a primary image URL. This API delivers only JSON. The request URL is:

```
https://api.harvardartmuseums.org/OBJECT?hasimage=1&title=garden&size=
20&apikey=YYYY
```

In other words, we are looking for the first 20 objects that have images with the word 'garden' in the title. At the end you add your own API key.

For the Finnish National Gallery we also need an API key (swap the ZZZZ in the code for your own key). Here there is no way of searching for artwork which contains an image URL in the result. The documentation promises a limit of 500 artworks, with no option of pagination. However, in reality there are never more than 100 results. The results are presented using the DC standard and can be delivered in JSON and XML.

```
http://kokoelmat.fng.fi/api/v2?&q=search:garden&format=dc-json&apikey=ZZZZ
```

The API request is for artworks that contain the word 'garden' (in this case it does not seem to make any difference to the results if we use the Finnish word for garden 'puutarha' instead), specifying JSON format and adding your own API key.

Step 2

Finding a search phrase that will retrieve similar artworks from all three sources was quite difficult, mostly due to language, despite the fact that all three collections have English titles as a part of their metadata.

At first, I wanted to find botanical artwork, and using the search-term 'botanical' gave good results in the Dutch and American APIs. However, the results in the Finnish API did not contain any images. A search for 'flower' in the Finnish API returned a suitable result. Using this term in the Dutch API returned more than ten images of the same 'Bloempiramide' (English: flower pyramid) and other furniture pieces with flowers on them. Finally, I used the search term 'garden' which gave similar results for each collection. Again, language proved to be a small issue, as the Dutch results also included an artwork named 'Uniformen van Gardes' (English: uniforms of the guards).

This example shows that when trying to combine sets of similar heritage data, mapping each dataset to the others is not straightforward. The greatest challenge was finding a search phrase that would return similar results from each collection. Even when all the collections contained English titles, this was an issue, due to documentation differences across institutions. What one institution calls 'botanical' is not the same as what another institution would call it. Further, mapping the datasets to each other showed how different search and naming conventions can create issues. For example, the fact that the Dutch API searches all metadata fields for the term meant that the result might be very different from that returned by the American API, which searches for the term only in the title fields. This illustrates how usable access to these datasets is reliant on a good documentation.

Once we have identified an appropriate search term we can use the URLs to request the dataset using the different JSON-formatted standards. Each set of numbered results is called something different: 'artObjects', 'records' and 'descriptionSet' (Table 6.1 opposite). Reaching the image URL is even more different. In the Dutch dataset this is kept in the 'URL' element under the 'webImage' element. For the American dataset it is kept in the 'primary imageURL' element and for the Finnish dataset it is kept in the 'URL' element, under the first (i.e. 0) element in the 'relation' element, if it exists at all. Apart from these three elements, which we will use in the following code, each dataset also returns other information. The Dutch dataset includes the artist. The American dataset includes the artist as well as the accession year, technique, date, copyright and more. The Finnish dataset also includes the artist, dates of acquisition and creation, subject, material and more. This means that we could also search across these three datasets for artworks made by a specific artist. However, if we wanted to search for art acquired in a particular year or wanted to present the datasets based on the date of acquisition, we would be able to include only the American and the Finnish datasets, as the Dutch collection search does not return this data. This can be accessed only through specific record searches.

Table 6.1 *Comparison of the Rijksmuseum, Harvard Art Museum and Finnish National Gallery APIs*

	Rijksmuseum (Dutch)	Harvard Art Museum (US)	Finnish National Gallery
API URL	https://www.rijksmuseum.nl/api/en	https://api.harvardartmuseums.org	http://kokoelmat.fng.fi/api/v2?
Method to access artwork	/collection?	/OBJECT?	q=search:word
API Key (yes/no)	yes (and Rijksstudio account)	yes	yes
Format	Use format=json	Always JSON	Use format=dc:json
Images	imgonly=true	Add hasimage=1	Cannot search for results with images only
Number of results	Default is 10, max is ps=100 (options for pagination)	Default is 10, max is size=100 (options for pagination)	Limit is 100 results with no pagination option
Query	q=garden	Can search only the title, title=*garden*	q=search:*garden*
Results path	->artObjects->[0]	->records->[0]	->descriptionSet->[0]
Results title	->title	->title	->title[2]->en
Results image URL	->webImage->URL	->primaryimageURL	->relation[0]->URL

Step 3

The PHP and HTML code below does the following.

1 For each of the three datasets (Rijksmuseum, Harvard Art Museum and Finnish National Gallery) the results are retrieved for one page of results.
2 The JSON results are decoded.
3 A div is created to contain each of the datasets.
4 It loops through the records in each dataset, outputting the title and the image URL as a part of an HTML <img> tag with a horizontal line (<hr/>) after each record.
5 The American and Finnish results include records both with and without images. To overcome this issue we could have included an 'if statement' specifying to print the item only if there is an image.

```
<?php
// Dataset 1: Rijksmuseum (Dutch)
// API URL
$api_URL1 =
'https://www.rijksmuseum.nl/api/en/collection?format=json&q=garden&imgonly=
```

```php
true&ps=20&key=XXXX';
// call the JSON file
$json_file1 = file_get_contents($api_URL1);
// decode JSON file into a PHP array
$resource_array1 = json_decode($json_file1);
// make div for column of images
echo "<div style='width:30%;float:left;'>";
// make header with title
echo '<h1>Rijksmuseum (Dutch)</h1>';
// loop through each record
foreach ($resource_array1->artObjects as $value1){
  // print the title
  echo $value1->title;
  // add line break
  echo "<br/>";
  // get the image URL
   $img1 = $value1->webImage->URL;
  // print image to 200px width
  echo ' <img width="200px" src="', $img1, '"/>';
  // add horizontal line
  echo "<hr/>";
} // loop end
echo "</div>";
// Dataset 2: Harvard Art Museum (American)
// API URL
$api_URL2 =
'https://api.harvardartmuseums.org/OBJECT?hasimage=1&title=garden&size=20&ap
ikey=YYYY';
// call the JSON file
$json_file2 = file_get_contents($api_URL2);
// decode JSON file into a PHP array
$resource_array2 = json_decode($json_file2);
// make div for column of images
echo "<div style='width:30%;float:left;'>";
// make header with title
echo '<h1>Harvard Art Museum (American)</h1>';
// loop through each record
foreach ($resource_array2->records as $value2){
  // Get the image URL
  $img2 = $value2->primaryimageURL;
  // if there is an image URL
  if($img2 !=""){
    // print the title
    echo $value2->title;
    // add line break
    echo "<br/>";
    // print image to 200px width
    echo ' <img width="200px" src="', $img2, '"/>';
    // add horizontal line
    echo "<hr/>";
  }
} // loop end
echo "</div>";
```

```php
// Dataset 3: Finnish National Gallery
// API URL
$api_URL3 = 'http://kokoelmat.fng.fi/api/v2?&q=search:garden&format=dc-
json&apikey=ZZZZ';
// call the JSON file
$json_file3 = file_get_contents($api_URL3);
// decode JSON file into a PHP array
$resource_array3 = json_decode($json_file3);
// make div for column of images
echo "<div style='width:30%;float:left;'>";
// make header with title
echo '<h1>Finnish National Gallery</h1>';
// loop through each record
foreach ($resource_array3->descriptionSet as $value3){
  // get the image URL
  $img3 = $value3->relation[0]->URL;
  // if there is an image URL
  if($img3 !=""){
    // print the title
    echo $value3->title[2]->en;
    // add line break
    echo "<br/>";
    // print image to 200px width
    echo ' <img width="200px" src="', $img3, '"/>';
    // add horizontal line
    echo "<hr/>";
  }
} // loop end
echo "</div>";
?>
```

Result

The result of this code is three columns, each with images and titles from one of the three institutions. In Figure 6.1 on the next page we can see that the search for the term 'garden' does not return similar results of images of actual gardens from all of the APIs. Only the Finnish National Gallery returns images of typical gardens.

Combining archaeological records

Archaeological excavations generate large amounts of data. For every ancient artefact painstakingly dug out of the ground, for every feature recognised, data is attached. Because of the destructive nature of archaeology, it is necessary that every important aspect is recorded for later analysis. Once the layer has been excavated, there is no going back: it is gone forever. What are left are the photographs, drawings, lists, descriptions and more. A large part of this data is the geographical aspect. Even before the archaeologist begins

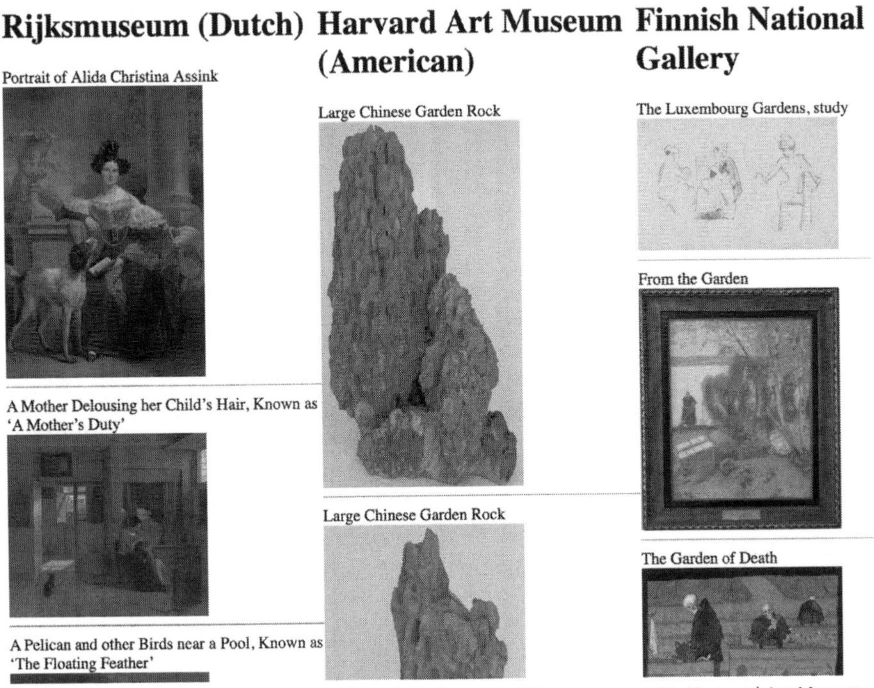

Rijksmuseum (Dutch)

Portrait of Alida Christina Assink

Harvard Art Museum (American)

Large Chinese Garden Rock

Finnish National Gallery

The Luxembourg Gardens, study

From the Garden

A Mother Delousing her Child's Hair, Known as 'A Mother's Duty'

Large Chinese Garden Rock

The Garden of Death

A Pelican and other Birds near a Pool, Known as 'The Floating Feather'

Figure 6.1 *Visualisation of images of gardens from the Rijksmuseum API, Harvard Art Museum API and Finnish National Gallery API*

to excavate, the location is examined in previous records, on maps and physically. In many countries around the world there are records of previous archaeological finds, monuments and known sites. In some countries, like Sweden, these finds and monument records are available to search through national portals like Swedish Open Cultural Heritage (SOCH) ('K-samsök' in Swedish; ksamsok.se), along with metadata from other Swedish heritage institutions. This metadata only scratches the surface of data gathered from archaeological excavations and finds, with only one set of coordinates per record. These coordinates are often attached to a historical or prehistoric time period, as well as a short description of the site. This example will use the SOCH API and combine this with records from the Open Context project, which is run by Sarah Whitcher Kansa and Eric Kansa under the Alexandria Archive Institute, an American non-profit heritage tech company, which edits, reviews and publishes heritage datasets in collaboration with the California Digital Library, University of California (cdlib.org). Open Context includes archaeological data from around the world. However, only one of the projects, the Biometrical Database of European Aurochs and Domestic Cattle, includes data points from Sweden. This is a dataset published (Wright et al., 2016) as part of Elizabeth Wright's PhD thesis exploring the morphological variation of the European aurochs (Bos primigenius) from the Middle Pleistocene to the medieval period. In this example I will combine the two datasets into a map of animal bone finds from the Swedish Stone Age (c. 13000–1700 BCE).

Step 1

The first step is to combine the parameters of the search for each URL. First is the Open Context dataset, which returns the data as JSON. As this dataset covers the whole world we first have to specify that we wish to retrieve the part of the dataset that is from Sweden. The API by default returns 20 records, with a max of 1000 (rows=1000). The Open Context dataset is searched for animal bones (prop=oc-gen-cat-animal-bone), from the Swedish Stone Age (form-start=-13000&form-stop=-1700), in the Wright project (proj=65-biometrical-database-of-european-aurochs-and-domestic-c). Open Context does not require an API key or registration before use.

```
https://opencontext.org/subjects-search/Sweden.json?rows=1000&form-start=-
13000&form-stop=-1700&proj=65-biometrical-database-of-european-aurochs-and-
domestic-c&prop=oc-gen-cat-animal-bone
```

SOCH does require an API key, which you get by emailing them (swap your key for XXXX in the code). The default hits retrieved is 12, with a max of 500 (hitsPerPage=500). The different requests are sent to the API in the query parameter with %20and%20 between each part (%20 is URL code for a space). The query requests the results with geographical coordinates (geoDataExists=j), from the Stone Age (Stenålder in Swedish, sten%C3%A5lder where %C3%A5 is URL code for å), about animal bones (djurben in Swedish). We want to retrieve the fields for the longitude and latitude coordinates (fields=lon,lat) and the dataset as XML (recordSchema=xml). Finally, the API key (x-api=XXXX) is sent too.

```
http://www.kulturarvsdata.se/ksamsok/api?method=search&hitsPerPage=500&
query=geoDataExists=j%20and%20sten%C3%A5lder%20and%20djurben&recordSchema=
xml&fields=lon,lat&x-api=XXXX
```

Step 2

The datasets that are retrieved through the two URLs above consist of 114 records of animal bones from around 12 different Swedish sites in Open Context and about 90 records of animal bones from different sites in SOCH. The latter data come from two Swedish sources (Riksantikvarieämbetet and Statens historiska museum) and reflect what is registered with geographical location in this database, and not necessarily all Swedish archaeology.

Step 3

The HTML and JavaScript code below does the following.

1   In the HTML head we link to the OL CSS style as well as writing our own CSS style to specify how high and wide we want our map.
2   We link to the OL code library so that we can use its commands (beginning with ol.).
3   We link to the jQuery code library in order to get and loop the JSON and XML datasets.
4   In the HTML body we add a div tag with the id 'map' – this is the same tag we styled above.
5   This next part is written in JavaScript code, where we first retrieve the two datasets using the getJSON() or get() functions and the each() function to loop the records.
6   For each record the coordinates are added to a point, which in turn is added to a pointsSource variable.
7   As the JSON data from Open Context also contains Polygons, we use an 'if statement' to filter so that we retrieve only the Points.
8   A variable called 'map' is created to hold the map data.
9   The map consists of three layers, the first being the map from OSM.
10 On top of this layer are the two data layers, which are each created through the pointsSource variables.
11 The two vector layers are styled with circles in different colours (green/blue for the Open Context points and pink/purple for the SOCH points).
12 Finally, we make a viewport for this map centred on the coordinates for Sweden (13.00, 58.00) and with the spatial reference set to WGS 84 (EPSG:4326) and WGS 84 Web Mercator (EPSG:3857).
13 The last thing we set is the beginning zoom of the map to 6. The higher the zoom number, the closer the map will zoom to begin with.

```
<html>
  <head>
    <!- HTML comment: link to openlayers CSS style ->
    <link rel="stylesheet"
href="https://cdn.rawgit.com/openlayers/openlayers.github.io/master/en/
v5.3.0/css/ol.css" type="text/css">
    <style>
      /* CSS comments - style the div container with the id=map */
      #map {
        height: 500px;
        width: 100%;
      }
    </style>
    <!- link to openlayers code library ->
```

```html
    <script
src="https://cdn.rawgit.com/openlayers/openlayers.github.io/master/en/
v5.3.0/build/ol.js"></script>
    <script src="https://code.jquery.com/jquery-3.4.1.js"></script>
  </head>
  <body>
    <!- div container for the map ->
    <div id="map" ></div>
    <!- JavaScript creating the map ->
    <script type="text/javascript">
      // create a variable for the points from dataset 1
        var pointsSource1 = new ol.source.Vector();
      // get the JSON dataset from Open Context
$.getJSON('https://opencontext.org/subjects-search/Sweden.json?rows=1000&
form-start=-13000&form-stop=-1700&proj=65-biometrical-database-of-european-
aurochs-and-domestic-c&prop=oc-gen-cat-animal-bone', function(json) {
  // for each of the features in the dataset
  $.each(json.features, function() {
  // if the geometry type is Point
  if (this.geometry.type ==="Point"){
    // create a variable for the points from dataset 1
    var points1 = new ol.Feature({
      // set the geometry for the points feature with the coordinates and the
spatial reference
        geometry: new
ol.geom.Point(ol.proj.transform([parseFloat(this.geometry.coordinates[0]),
parseFloat(this.geometry.coordinates[1])], 'EPSG:4326', 'EPSG:3857')),
      }); // end of point creation
    // add each new point to the source variable
    pointsSource1.addFeature(points1);
    } // end of if condition
  }); // end of feature loop
}); // end of JSON function

// create a variable for the points from dataset 2
var pointsSource2 = new ol.source.Vector();
// get the XML dataset from K-samsök
$.get('http://www.kulturarvsdata.se/ksamsok/api?method=search&hitsPerPage=50
0&query=geoDataExists=j%20and%20sten%C3%A5lder%20and%20djurben&recordSchema=
xml&fields=lon,lat&x-api=XXXX',function(xml) {
  // for each of the records in the dataset
  $('record', xml).each(function () {
    // create a variable for the points from dataset 2
    var points2 = new ol.Feature({
      // set the geometry for the points feature with the coordinates and
the spatial reference
        geometry: new
ol.geom.Point(ol.proj.transform([parseFloat($(this).find('field[name="lon"]'
).text()), parseFloat($(this).find('field[name="lat"]').text())],
'EPSG:4326', 'EPSG:3857')),
      }); // end of point creation
    // add each new point to the source variable
    pointsSource2.addFeature(points2);
    }); // end of feature loop
}); // end of XML function

//  create a new map in the variable "map"
var map = new ol.Map({
// place the map in the div container with the id = map
```

```
target: 'map',
  // create layers:
  layers: [
  // add the Open Street Map (OSM) as the first layer
    new ol.layer.Tile({

      source: new ol.source.OSM()
    }), // end of first layer

    // add the JSON file from Open Context as the second layer
    new ol.layer.Vector({
      // use the variable pointsSource1 as the source
      source: pointsSource1,
      // style the second layer
      style: new ol.style.Style({
        // style each point as a circle
        image: new ol.style.Circle({
          radius: 8,
          fill: new ol.style.Fill({
            color: 'green'
          }),
          // style the circle edge
          stroke: new ol.style.Stroke({
          color: 'blue',
            width: 1
          })
        }),
      }) // end of style
    }), // end of layer 2

    // add the XML file from K-samsök as the third layer
    new ol.layer.Vector({
      // use the variable pointsSource1 as the source
      source: pointsSource2,
      // style the third layer
      style: new ol.style.Style({
        // style each point as a circle
        image: new ol.style.Circle({
        radius: 8,
        fill: new ol.style.Fill({
          color: 'pink'
        }),
        // style the circle edge
        stroke: new ol.style.Stroke({
          color: 'purple',
          width: 1
        })
      }),
    }) // end of style
  })], // end of layer 3 and the layers

  // set the viewport of the map
  view: new ol.View({
  //center on the coordinates for Sweden (-6.400000, 53.320000) and set the
```

```
spatial references to WGS 84 (EPSG:4326) and WGS 84 Web Mercator (EPSG:3857)
    center: ol.proj.transform([13.00, 58.00], 'EPSG:4326', 'EPSG:3857'),
    // set the map zoom - the higher the number the more the map zooms in.
        zoom: 6
    }) // end of view
}); // end of map
    </script>
  </body>
</html>
```

Result

Figure 6.2 shows the result of this code: a map centred on Sweden with the 12 find spots for animal bones from Open Context in dark grey and the approximately 90 find spots from SOCH in light grey.

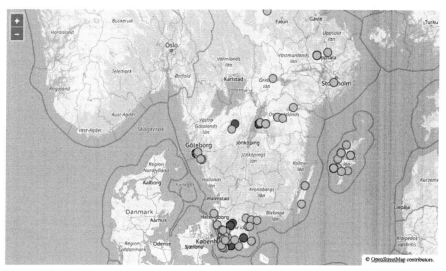

Figure 6.2 *A map of animal bones from the Swedish Stone Age. Data from Open Context API (dark grey) and Swedish Open Cultural Heritage API (light grey), CC BY*

Combining newspapers

As mentioned previously, there is a longer history of combining library records compared to the rest of the GLAM sector. This is because of the obvious usefulness and profitability in library records, and this is also the reason why it is very difficult to get hold of library catalogue data as open data. Often these datasets have APIs that are used for internal development by companies specialising in library management software. In other words, where most heritage institutions are trying hard to get people to use their datasets for new and exciting ventures, libraries already have software developers using their datasets, and have done so for years. This is mostly the case for material that is still in use, but many national and university libraries also have heritage material that is not part of the main library catalogue. This material is beginning to be published online as open data, and one aspect of this is the digitisation and OCR conversion of historical newspapers. In the following example we will use newspapers from two open collections to create a chart of mentions of Mahatma Gandhi in the 1920s. We are again using the chartist.js library to create the chart.

Step 1

The first dataset is from Europeana and has 369 results in a search for 'Mahatma Gandhi' mentions in newspapers from Germany (319), Estonia (26), Latvia (23) and Poland (1) between 1920 and 1929. This API requires an API key, which is easy to sign up for on the Europeana Pro site (swap your key for XXXX in the following code).

```
https://newspapers.eanadev.org/api/v2/search.json?query=mahatma+gandhi&rows=
100&profile=hits&wskey=XXXX&qf=proxy_dcterms_issued:%5B1920-01-01+TO+1929-
12-31%5D
```

The number of results that are returned through the Europeana API is 12 by default and has a maximum of 100 results (rows=100) from one call. This means that the code must include more than one call to the API in order to return all 369 results. The further URL calls to the Europeana API are made by adding the parameter 'start=101' to the URL to offset the results by 100 for each new call. We want data from the 1920s only, so we need to specify this too (qf=proxy_dcterms_issued:%5B1920-01-01+TO+1929-12-31%5D).

The second dataset is from National Library of Australia (Trove) and has 458 results in a search for 'Mahatma Gandhi' mentions in Australian newspapers between 1920 and 1929. Again, this resource requires an API key, which can be retrieved from the Trove help centre (swap your key for YYYY in the code).

```
https://api.trove.nla.gov.au/v2/result?q=mahatma+gandhi%20&zone=newspaper&
n=100&encoding=json&key=YYYY&l-decade=192
```

As with the first dataset, Trove also returns a maximum of 100 (n=100) results. Again, we need to use pagination in order to send further URL calls to retrieve the next sets of results. The Trove API includes a URL that points to the next set of 100 results. Finally, we want to retrieve data from the 1920s only (l-decade=192).

Step 2

The results of the two API calls to Europeana and Trove returned newspapers in five different languages (English, German, Estonian, Latvian and Polish). This is also the reason why I decided to search for a person's name that was likely to occur during this period (i.e. Mahatma Gandhi). A search for an object or concept would not be as successful because I would have to translate it into all the possible languages in the APIs, which in the case of Europeana include many European languages besides English. This is an issue when using the dataset too, and therefore the following chart will make use of only the newspapers' year of issue. This example shows that even in cases where language provides a substantial barrier we can still make use of OHD in a meaningful way (see Chapter 7 for a further use of the Trove dataset for research purposes).

Step 3:

The PHP, JavaScript and HTML code below does the following.

- It calls up the datasets, one at a time, and creates a loop through the sets of 100 results, based on the total number of results.
- It loops through each record and extracts the date and the year from the first four digits of the date.
- The dates are added to one array called $year_array, with a separate percentage of the results for each year in the two datasets (i.e. percentage-EU and percentage-Trove).
- The $year_array is sorted in ascending order by years.
- In the HTML head the chartist.js code library and stylesheet are called.
- In the HTML body a div is created with the class 'ct-chart' and 'ct-major-twelfth'. The latter is one of several predefined chartist.js aspect ratios to choose between.
- In the JavaScript the data for the labels (x-axis) and series (y-axis) is pulled from the PHP $year_array using a PHP foreach loop. The series uses the percentages from both datasets.
- The option settings specify that the y-axis must use whole numbers with a percentage sign after.
- The Chartist.Bar() function is called, adding the data and options to the div with the class 'ct-chart'.

```php
<?php
// Dataset 1: Europeana newspapers
// API URL
$ap1_URL1 =
'https://newspapers.eanadev.org/api/v2/search.json?query=mahatma+gandhi&rows
```

```
=100&profile=hits&wskey=XXXX&qf=proxy_dcterms_issued:%5B1920-01-01+TO+1929-
12-31%5D';
// call the JSON file the first time
$json_file1 = file_get_contents($api_URL1);
// decode JSON file into a PHP array
$resource_array1 = json_decode($json_file1);
// get the total results
$total1=$resource_array1->totalResults;
// loop through the result sets
for ($x = 0; $x <= $total1; $x+=100) {
  // loop through each record
  foreach ($resource_array1->items as $value1){
    // get the date
    $titlestr = $value1->title[0];
    $date1 = substr($titlestr, -10);
    // get the year from the first 4 digits
    $year1 = substr($date1, 0, 4);
    // build an array for each year and percentage for Europeana
    $year_array[$year1]['year'] = $year1;
    // add +1 to the count of each year when it occurs
    $year_array[$year1]['amount-EU'] += 1;
    // calculate the percentage of each year in the records
    $year_array[$year1]['percentage-EU'] =
round($year_array[$year1]['amount-EU']/$total1*100, 2);
  } // end result loop
  // add 101 to count
  $x1=$x+101;
  // create the new URL for the next set
  $next1
="https://newspapers.eanadev.org/api/v2/search.json?query=mahatma+gandhi&row
s=100&profile=hits&wskey=XXXX&qf=proxy_dcterms_issued:%5B1920-01-01+TO+1929-
12-31%5D";
  $api_URL1=$next1.'&start='.$x1;
  // call the new JSON file
  $json_file1 = file_get_contents($api_URL1);
  // decode the new JSON file into a PHP array
  $resource_array1 = json_decode($json_file1);
} // end set loop

// Dataset 2: Trove newspapers
// API URL
$api_URL2 =
'https://api.trove.nla.gov.au/v2/result?q=mahatma+gandhi&zone=newspaper&n=10
0&encoding=json&key=YYYY&l-decade=192';
// call the JSON file
$json_file2 = file_get_contents($api_URL2);
// decode JSON file into a PHP array
$resource_array2 = json_decode($json_file2);
// get the total results
$total2=$resource_array2->response->zone[0]->records->total;
// loop through the result sets
for ($x = 0; $x <= $total2; $x+=100) {
  // loop through each record
```

```php
  foreach ($resource_array2->response->zone[0]->records->article as
$value2){
    // get the date
    $date2 = $value2->date;
    // get the year from the first 4 digits
    $year2 = substr($date2, 0, 4);
    // build an array for each year and percentage for Trove
    $year_array[$year2]['year'] = $year2;
     // add +1 to the count of each year when it occurs
    $year_array[$year2]['amount-Trove'] += 1;
    // Calculate the percentage of each year in the records
     $year_array[$year2]['percentage-Trove'] =
round($year_array[$year2]['amount-Trove']/$total2*100, 2);
  } // end result Loop
  // create the new URL for the next set
  $next2 = $resource_array2->response->zone[0]->records->next;
  $api_URL2='https://api.trove.nla.gov.au/v2/'.$next2.'&key=YYYY';
  // call the new JSON file
  $json_file2 = file_get_contents($api_URL2);
  // decode the new JSON file into a PHP array
  $resource_array2 = json_decode($json_file2);
}
// sort the years in ascending order
asort($year_array);
?>

<!DOCTYPE html>
<html>
  <head>
  <!-- links to Chartist code library and stylesheet -->
    <link rel="stylesheet"
href="//cdn.jsdelivr.net/chartist.js/latest/chartist.min.css">
    <script
src="//cdn.jsdelivr.net/chartist.js/latest/chartist.min.js"></script>
  </head>
  <body>
    <!-- add div for chart using predefined Chartist classes-->
    <div class="ct-chart ct-major-twelfth"></div>
<script type="text/javascript">
  // start of JS script
  // chart build - gather the data
  var data = {
    // create labels (x-axis)
    labels: [
<?php
// in PHP build a comma separated list of years
foreach ($year_array as $value){
    echo "'" . $value['year'] . "',";}
?> // end of php
    ],
    // create series with 2 bars for each year (y-axis)
    series: [[
<?php
```

```
  foreach ($year_array as $value){
    echo "" . $value['percentage-EU'] . ",";}
?> // end of php
    ],[
<?php
  foreach ($year_array as $value){
    echo "" . $value['percentage-Trove'] . ",";}
?> // end of php
    ]]
  };

  var options = {
    // options for the y-axis
    axisY: {
      // no decimal numbers
      onlyInteger: true,
      labelInterpolationFnc: function(value) {
        // add percentage sign to the numbers
        return value + '%';
      }
    }
  };
  // create the chart in the div with the ct-chart class, using the data and
the options above
  new Chartist.Bar('.ct-chart', data, options);
  // end of  JS script
</script>
  </body>
</html>
```

Results

Figure 6.3 shows the bar chart displaying the years from 1920 to 1929 along the x-axis and the percentage of each dataset for each year along the y-axis. In other words, a visualisation of the percentage of mentions per year of

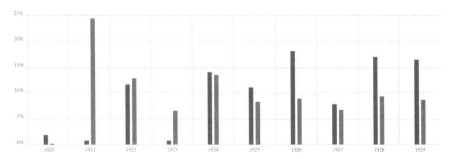

Figure 6.3 *A bar chart showing mentions of Mahatma Gandhi in the 1920s, by year. Data from Europeana API (left) and Trove API (right). CC BY*

Mahatma Gandhi in the 1920s in, respectively, European and Australian newspapers. The European percentages are displayed in the darker bar to the left and the Australian in the lighter bars to the right. It is important to note that this is just an example of how these datasets can be visualised, and that it probably does not reflect the actual mentions of Gandhi in European or Australian newspapers. We simply know too little about the reliability and completeness of the datasets to make any such claims (see Chapter 7).

Summary

This chapter has:

1 illustrated how to combine images retrieved from three different Art Museums (the Dutch Rijksmuseum, the US Harvard Art Museum and the Finnish National Gallery) for the search term 'garden'. Each request is different, as the three museums use different API styles and different standards. The code retrieves the image URLs from each API and displays the artworks side by side.

2 illustrated how to combine coordinates from two archaeological datasets (the SOCH portal and the Open Context project) for a search for animal bones from the Stone Age. The two APIs return data in different formats (XML and JSON) as well as different standards. The code retrieves the longitude and latitude of each find and displays the points on a map using different colours.

3 illustrated how to combine metadata from two newspaper datasets (Europeana and the National Library of Australia (Trove)) for a search for the mention of 'Mahatma Gandhi' in the 1920s. The two APIs return datasets in different languages (English, Estonian, German, Latvian and Polish), making it difficult to combine the text of the newspaper articles. The code therefore retrieves the years when the newspapers were published and displays these dates in a chart of percentages of mentions per year for each dataset.

## 7

Open data for research

Data science is making its way into the humanities, slowly but surely. Some researchers have been working with heritage datasets for a while but, overall, adoption of analysis based on more structured datasets has been slow in the arts and humanities. As with heritage institutions, it is often due to a lack of skill and perhaps a propensity to theorise about data rather than delve into datasets themselves.

While open data can serve as a means to engage and create new narratives of heritage among the public, it also has a large role to play in research. Today some funding agencies encourage open datasets as a part of the projects they fund, alongside open access publication. An example of this is the EU's Horizon 2020 programme, which encourages open access to research data, although opt-outs are possible. It is guided by the principle of 'as open as possible, as closed as necessary' (European Commission, 2019). In some research subjects the publication of datasets alongside research publications plays an important role in order to allow other researchers to replicate studies. We do not have a tradition of this in the heritage field. However, as more research comes to be based on larger datasets this will, hopefully, become an important part of research publication. Further, access to open heritage datasets will enable researchers to try out these methods on even more datasets.

An example of this is the project Six Degrees of Francis Bacon, which is a digital reconstruction of an early modern social network. The dataset is visualised on the website in such a way that it can be explored by any researcher or student. Further, the dataset and visualisations are licensed under a CC BY-NC-SA licence, allowing anyone to use them for any non-commercial purpose. This is a step forward, but at the same time not enough, as the use of non-commercial licences is not fully open (see Chapter 2).

This chapter will show an example of using open datasets for research purposes. While the use of these methods in the humanities has become more common over the years, applying them to open heritage datasets is still in its infancy generally.

I will use Python instead of PHP and JavaScript to demonstrate how to use open data for research purposes. Further, I will use one dataset for all the coding examples, in this case, Trove.

Trove (National Library of Australia) is probably the best-documented and most user-friendly example of a heritage data API that we have to date. Much of this is due to the tireless work of Tim Sherratt, who was Trove manager from 2013 to 2016. He is currently an Associate Professor of Digital Heritage at the University of Canberra, Australia. However, through the GLAM Workbench (glam-workbench.github.io) he continues to teach everyone and anyone how to work with heritage data, including Trove.

The GLAM Workbench is a collection of Jupyter notebooks (i.e. coding environments for Python) aimed at showing how to explore and use data from GLAM institutions. GLAM Workbench is licensed with a CC BY licence and includes tutorials from getting started with notebooks to walk-throughs of using various GLAM collections, much like this book's Chapters 5 and 6 but with Python. The tutorials for Trove data are the most in-depth, and I have personally learnt a lot from working through them. If you wish to delve deeper into data analysis with Python and heritage datasets after this chapter, I would highly recommend that you have a look at the GLAM Workbook. One other reason for this choice is that Trove includes a facet search option where you can extract full datasets for a particular facet (e.g. year or title) and can in this way bypass the limits on the number of full records (i.e. max 100 records).

The following tutorials are inspired by the GLAM Workbench and other online resources to show how to do basic data collection, data cleaning, descriptive statistics and timeline analysis with Python. This is also an example of the creative coding practices of combining code from various sources and building on what has come before.

I will freely admit that the whole concept of data science using Python for data analysis is pretty new to me. This is all the more reason for readers to trust me when I say that if I can delve into this, so can they. Of course, one has to approach new methods with caution and take great care to understand the limits and caveats for those methods. On the other hand, I would encourage you to be brave and take a leap into, for example, a simple data analysis with the different datasets available.

The tutorial is based on the following research question:

When did Australian newspapers mention Indian lawyer, politician and social activist Mahatma Gandhi (1869–1948) and is there a connection to notable events in his political work?

Basic data collection

As in Chapter 5, I will begin with the basics of data collection from a heritage API using Python, the Python data analysis code library Pandas and the Requests code library. In the following I will run one code section at a time and describe the result. Comments in the code are denoted with a hashtag at the beginning. See Appendix B for an introduction to Python.

Step 1

The first step is to import any code libraries needed. The Requests coding library enables the HTTP requests to the API, rather than putting together a URL as we did in Chapters 5 and 6. Pandas is a coding library which enables high-performance data analysis in Python. JSON Normalize is a Pandas function used to flatten JSON object structure to a Python dataframe (like a table) structure.

```
# first import the Requests library1
import requests
# import the Pandas library and add to alias 'pd'
import pandas as pd
# import the JSON normalize module from Pandas1
from pandas.io.json import json_normalize
```

Step 2

This next code sets up the request in a similar fashion to the URLs used to retrieve data in Chapter 5. Trove requires an API key to return data. You can apply for your own key in the Trove help centre and use it to replace the 'XXXX' in the code.

A second variable sets the search URL for the Trove API, and then a Python dictionary sets the various parameters that we will use to call the API and return a JSON dataset of counts of mentions of Mahatma Gandhi per year in Australian newspapers. The + in the phrase 'mahatma+gandhi' is used to denote a space. Whether the phrase is in capital letters or not makes no difference. The zone parameter specifies that we want the result to include newspapers only. For the key parameter we use the 'api_key' variable. Facets=year and n=0 requests only the dataset divided into years and not any individual records like in Chapter 6. We retrieve the response through the 'requests.get' function, where we send the dictionary of parameters and the URL.

```
# a variable called 'api_key', paste your key between the quotes
api_key - 'XXXX'
```

```
# a variable for the API URL - note that we are using v2 - version 2
api_search_URL = 'https://api.trove.nla.gov.au/v2/result'

# a dictionary called 'params' setting the parameters we will send to the
API
params = {
 'q': 'mahatma+gandhi',
 'zone': 'newspaper',
 'key': api_key,
 'facet': 'year',
 'encoding': 'json',
 'n': 0
}
# retrieves the response for the URL and parameters we are sending
response = requests.get(api_search_URL, params=params)
# response status code - 200 means request was successful
response.status_code
```

The result of this is a status code 200, which tells us that the request was successful and that our data is now stored in the variable 'response'.

Step 3

The third and last step of this basic example is to make a JSON dictionary of the response and to flatten the facet results from this JSON file into a Pandas dataframe 'df'. Whereas JSON is a good data exchange format based on lists of values or key/value pairs, it is not ideal for data analysis. The dataframe, on the other hand, is a two-dimensional, table-like structure with columns and rows, making it better suited to analysing large amounts of similar data in one go.

The structure of the returned JSON has the years and the count for each year in a list in the object 'term', which we have to dig down to in order to retrieve this dataset. Finally, we can print the dataframe (df) and view the result.

```
# convert response into a JSON dictionary
json = response.json()

# flatten the JSON file object "term" into a dataframe called df
df = json_normalize(json['response']['zone'][0]['facets']['facet']['term'])

# print the dataframe
print(df)
```

The result of this code is a table with two columns for the years ('display' and 'search'), the count of the amount of times the search term occurred each year and a URL to the results for that year (Table 7.1 opposite).

Table 7.1 *The original result of the Trove request as a dataframe/table*

count	display	search	URL	
0	1	2015	2015	/result?q=mahatma%2Bgandhi&facet=year&encoding...
1	1	2013	2013	/result?q=mahatma%2Bgandhi&facet=year&encoding...
2	1	2012	2012	/result?q=mahatma%2Bgandhi&facet=year&encoding...
3	2	2011	2011	/result?q=mahatma%2Bgandhi&facet=year&encoding...
4	2	2010	2010	/result?q=mahatma%2Bgandhi&facet=year&encoding...

Data cleaning

One of the bigger issues in terms of data and datasets, not only in heritage, is that data can be quite messy. Therefore an important step before data analysis is so-called data cleaning (Agarwal, 2017). This entails making sure that the data types for each column are appropriate to the type of data in that column; deleting columns that are not useful, or rows with faulty or no data; renaming rows and columns; and changing the index. The biggest task of all may be to detect and resolve cases of missing values in the data. There are different reasons for missing values; for example, the user forgetting to, or choosing not to, fill out the field, or data being lost due to data transfer or a programming error.

In the following we will use the code from the steps in the basic example to retrieve the same dataset for newspaper mentions of Mahatma Gandhi separated into years. The data cleaning will thus begin with step 4.

Step 4

In this step we first check which data types are in each column in the original dataframe (df). It turns out that while the columns containing years ('display' and 'search') quite rightly have the datatype integer (i.e. a whole number), the column for the count and the URL are objects (a string or text). This is okay for the URL column, which contains a string of various characters. However, if we later want to analyse the count as the numbers they are, the data type must also be set to integer.

Here I have used the Pandas function 'pd.to_numeric', which changes the data type into a numerical type (as a decimal or a whole number, depending on the data provided).

```
# Check the datatypes
df.dtypes

# change count to numeric
df['count'] = pd.to_numeric(df['count'])
```

Step 5

In this step we will remove the columns that are not useful for our further analysis. In this case we have no need for the URL column or for a second column with the same years. The Pandas 'drop' function is used to get rid of the two columns listed as the first parameter. The 'inplace' parameter instructs the drop to happen in the existing dataframe and 'axis=1' tells the function to drop the columns and not the rows with this index (i.e. axis=0).

```
# drop the columns 'search' and 'URL' in the dataframe
df.drop(['search', 'URL'], inplace=True, axis=1)
```

Step 6

We now have two columns left: 'count' and 'display'. The 'display' column contains our years, but the term 'display' does not indicate this well. Therefore we can rename this column to something like 'year'.

We do this by using the Pandas 'rename' function with an internal mapper function specifying that the columns 'display' must become 'year'. Again, the parameter 'inplace=True' is used to indicate that this must all happen in the current dataframe rather than by copying the result to a new dataframe.

```
# rename the column "display" to "year"
df.rename(columns={'display':'year'}, inplace=True)
```

The result of step 5 and 6 combined is a table-like dataframe with an index column and a column for the count of each mention of Mahatma Gandhi in newspapers for the corresponding year in the third column (Table 7.2).

Descriptive statistics

Statistical analysis has not been widely favoured in the humanities. Some subjects, like archaeology, have taken a turn towards using methods from 'the natural sciences', which speaks loudly of how out of place statistics can be in this environment. To be fair, most source material in the humanities does not lend

Table 7.2 *The dataframe after cleaning*

	count	year
0	1	2015
1	1	2013
2	1	2012
3	2	2011
4	2	2010

itself to statistical analysis, based on its limited volume and unstructured nature. Using a statistical model to analyse and describe five sources can seem senseless. However, digitisation of heritage material provides new opportunities for relevant and meaningful statistical analysis.

Again, we follow on from the steps in the two examples above. Having called and cleaned our Trove dataset we can now use the Pandas functions to analyse it more closely. This also includes statistics on the 'count' column, as we have transformed this into the numerical data type integer.

Step 7

We start by using the built-in function 'describe' to generate some basic descriptive statistics on the dataset, summarising the central tendency, dispersion and shape of the dataset's distribution. In other words, we will learn about the numerical columns with this simple function, but only the numerical columns.

```
# check the basic descriptive statistics
df.describe()
```

Table 7.3 shows the results of the 'describe' function, with a column of descriptive statistics for each of the two dataframe columns, 'count' and 'year'. In this case the count of each column is 89, meaning that there are no empty values. We have mentions of Mahatma Gandhi in Australian newspapers over 89 years, according to this dataset. Taking the year column first, the records begin in 1919 and end in 2015. The rest of the measurements for years make little sense. The counts of mentions of Mahatma Gandhi during the years go as low as 1 mention and as high as 898 mentions in one year. The mean is 102.8 mentions per year, with 50% of the counts being under 20 and 75% being around or under 113, meaning that more years had a low count of mentions and very few had mentions in the hundreds.

Table 7.3 *Descriptive statistics for the two columns in the dataframe*

	count	year
count	89	89
mean	102.8	1963.5
std	177.6	26.7
min	1	1919
25%	9	1941
50%	19	1963
75%	133	1985
max	898	2015

Timeline analysis

Samoilenko et al. (2017) explore how Wikipedia can be used as a data source for historiography. In their example the authors use the Wikipedia API to extract data from Wikipedia (which is openly accessible) to create a timeline comparison of the history of the 193 UN countries across the 30 biggest language Wikipedia editions. In other words, the dataset contains a description of each country's history on Wikipedia. This amasses to a dataset of approximately 17 million dates from across 773,121 articles. Their conclusions are that there is a 'recency bias' where most of the dates used in these Wikipedia articles are from more recent periods of history. Further, there is a strong focus on the history of European countries. This is not very surprising, given that they analyse only European languages, and years rather than time periods. But it is very interesting to see how they can use this method of analysis to show how Wikipedians focus on the history of conflict where particular gaps and bias exist. The authors conclude that they hope this awareness can benefit those who are seeking historical knowledge from Wikipedia (Samoilenko et al., 2017).

This is an example of the potential power of timeline analysis of larger heritage datasets. Through this method we can discover patterns and potential bias that is invisible through a closer reading of the same source material. We will now try to use this for our cleaned dataset in order to further understand when Australian newspapers mentioned Mahatma Gandhi.

Step 8

The next step here is to create a graph that illustrates clearly the relationship between the two columns in our dataframe (years and counts for each year). I am choosing to do this with a line chart, where the peaks and dips in the dataset become clear. For this we need a chart code library, and here we will use altair-viz.github.io, a code library for statistical visualisation. The line chart is created using the 'mark_line' function, with the parameter point=True. This visualises the dataset as a line with the points for each data value visible. Years go on the x-axis as a quantitative datatype (Q) and are displayed without decimals (format=c). The title for the x-axis is 'Year'. The counts for each year go on the y-axis, also encoded as a quantitative datatype (Q) and with the axis title 'Number of articles'. Finally, we close off the function by determining the size of the graph, in this case 700 pixels wide and 300 pixels high.

```
# import the altair code library
import altair as alt

# create a line plot
alt.Chart(df).mark_line(point=True).encode(
  # years go on the X axis
  x=alt.X('year:Q', axis=alt.Axis(format='c', title='Year')),
```

```
# number of articles go on the Y axis
y=alt.Y('count:Q', axis=alt.Axis(title='Number of articles')),

# determine the width and height of the graph
).properties(width=700, height=300)
```

Figure 7.1 shows a graph which can be saved as a PNG (Portable Network Graphics) image or an SVG (Scalable Vector Graphic), as well as opened in an editor. On this graph we can see that mentions of Mahatma Gandhi began in Australian newspapers only around the 1920s, with a sudden peak in 1931, then peaking regularly until 1948, after which they tapered out to a few articles each year. If we took this dataset and graph as it were, it would seem to suggest that mentions of Mahatma Gandhi in Australian newspapers began in 1919, when the *satyagraha* (civil disobedience) against the British in India began and Gandhi was arrested in April. The peak in 1931 coincides with the Gandhi-Irwin Pact in March, which came about through negotiations between Gandhi and the then Viceroy and Governor-General of India. The last peak, in 1948, coincides with the assassination of Gandhi (Gandhi Heritage Portal, 2019). After this, mentions of Mahatma Gandhi fade to a few each year.

All in all, it we can conclude from this that there is a connection between Australian newspapers' mention of Mahatma Gandhi and some of the more notable events in his political work.

This seems like a simple and neat way of understanding the history of Gandhi through newspapers, but there are several issues that we need to be aware of.

When using OHD or any digitised heritage datasets for historical research it is important to remember that the digitisation itself is a historical construction. Tim Sherratt reminds us of this with an example from the Trove

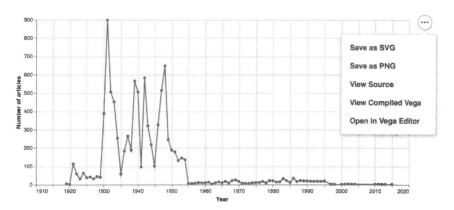

Figure 7.1 *Graph of mentions of 'Mahatma Gandhi' in Australian newspapers, by year. Data from Trove API, CC BY*

newspapers. A graph of digitised newspapers in Trove per year shows a very distinct peak around 1914–15.

'Yes, it's because of the war, but not in the way you might think. The peak is a result of digitisation priorities – in the lead up to the centenary of World War I it was decided to focus on digitising newspapers from the war period. If digitisation continues (and that's dependent on continued funding), the peak will disappear' (Sherratt, 2019b). In other words, there will be a larger number of results from the periods with more newspapers digitised. One way of counterbalancing this is to extract the year counts for articles in the newspaper and use these to calculate our counts of Mahatma Gandhi mentions as a proportion of the total number of articles for each year. This provides a different, but perhaps still not accurate, result for the actual mentions of Mahatma Gandhi over the years. Sherratt reminds us that 'the structure and content of a large corpus like Trove is not natural. While viewing the number of results over time can alert us to historical shifts, we have to be prepared to ask questions about how those results are generated, and what they represent' (Sherratt, 2019a).

The newspaper digitisation process involved OCR, which is a process that extracts the full text from the page images. In no way is this a perfect process, giving inconsistencies and errors in the finished result which in some cases Trove users have attempted to correct (Sherratt, 2019a). Furthermore, early newspapers are printed on lower-quality paper and with less OCR-friendly fonts. For example, there is a mention of 'Gandhis' in the Sydney *Daily Telegraph* on 6 April 1888, which upon closer inspection actually says 'and his'. In other words, the graph above represents the mentions of Mahatma Gandhi as understood by OCR, but not necessarily exactly what is printed.

The last issue has nothing to do with the digitisation as such but, rather, the original sources or lack of knowledge thereof. In this example I am using Australian newspapers because of the access to elements like years for an entire dataset, rather than retrieving records 100 at a time. But, in reality, I have little knowledge about Australian newspapers and news coverage of Mahatma Gandhi during his lifetime. A first search for the term 'Gandhi' alone returned 62,294 newspaper records beginning in 1855, a good 14 years before his birth in 1869 as Mohandas Karamchand Gandhi. This means that a search for 'Gandhi' would not actually return results for Mahatma Gandhi. I could also search for 'Mohandas Gandhi', which returns 423 results starting in 1914. This is rather less than the 7999 results for 'Mahatma Gandhi', which begin only five years later, in 1919. This is despite the honorific Mahātmā being applied to him in 1914 in South Africa, where he worked as a lawyer from 1893 to 1914 before returning to India to join the Independence movement in 1915 (Gandhi Heritage Portal, 2019).

Thus, I am not convinced that my search terms or the dataset from Trove are enough to give a firm answer to my research questions. However, this very simple example illustrates the power of combining OHD and data science. Imagine the alternative – travelling to Australia to go through millions of newspapers stored in different archives and libraries. This would be an impossible feat for me alone. OHD opens up the opportunity to ask and answer these types of questions from the comfort of my own desk, no matter who I am or where I live.

Summary

This chapter has:

1   discussed the role of OHD in humanities research and data science.
2   illustrated how to perform basic data collection and cleaning of live data from Australia's digitised newspapers through Trove using Python.
3   demonstrated how it is possible to extract descriptive statistics and visualise a timeline as a line-plot of the Trove dataset using Python.
4   discussed the validity of timeline analysis in relation to the digitisation process of Trove, such as the quality of OCR scanning and decisions taken about the focus of digitisation projects.

Appendix A: Examples used in the book

Institution/name
  Link
Arab Image Foundation
  arabimagefoundation.com
Archives New Zealand
  archives.govt.nz
Art Institute of Chicago
  artic.edu
Art Museum of Estonia Digital Collection
  kunstimuuseum.ekm.ee
Art Stories Faces
  artstories.it/en/faces
Ask a slave
  askaslave.com
Auckland Museum
  aucklandmuseum.com
Australian Lesbian and Gay Archives
  alga.org.au
Chronicling America
  chroniclingamerica.loc.gov
Culture Collage
  zenlan.com/collage
Culture Moves
  culturemoves.eu
Danish Demographic Database
  ddd.dda.dk
Danish Family Search
  danishfamilysearch.dk
Danish Netarchives
  netarkivet.dk

DIGIBÍS
  digibis.com
Digital Public Library of America
  dp.la
Europeana
  europeana.eu
Europeana Colour Explorer
  culturepics.org/colour
Finna
  finna.fi
Finnish National Gallery
  kansallisgalleria.fi
Flickr
  flickr.com
GLAM Workbench
  glam-workbench.github.io
Greetings from Zagreb
  pozdravizhrvatske.nsk.hr/zagrebapp
Hack4DK
  hack4.dk
Hackathon Bandung
  https://web.archive.org/web/20190528143217/http:/
  hackathonbandung.com/concept/.
Harvard Art Museum
  harvardartmuseums.org
Harvard Library
  library.harvard.edu
Hirschsprung Collection
  hirschsprung.dk
Internet Archive
  archive.org
Kolding Stadsarkiv
  stadsarkiv.kolding.dk
Lancashire Online Parish Clerks
  lan-opc.org.uk
Les Archives Nationales
  archives-nationales.culture.gouv.fr
Library of Congress
  loc.gov
Los Angeles County Museum
  lacma.org

Metropolitan Museum of Art
  metmuseum.org
Mikkelsen father and son
Museums Victoria Collections
  collections.museumvictoria.com.au
National Digital Library of India
  ndl.iitkgp.ac.in
National Gallery of Denmark
  smk.dk
National Library of Norway
  nb.no
Natural History Museum Vienna
  nhm-wien.ac.at
Nina Frances Layard
No Gun Ri Digital Archive
  nogunri.rit.albany.edu
On this day
  culturepics.org/on-this-day
Open Context
  opencontext.org
Open Data DK
  opendata.dk
Open Street Map
  openstreetmap.org
openAfrica
  africaopendata.org
PoetryDB
  poetrydb.org
Portable Antiquities Scheme
  finds.org.uk
Post & Tele Museum
  ptt-museum.dk
Querypic
  dhistory.org/querypic
Rijksmuseum
  rijksmuseum.nl
Skagen Art Museum
  skagenskunstmuseer.dk
Smithsonian
  si.edu

South Dublin County Council
  http://heritagewalks.sdcc.ie
Spoonflower
  spoonflower.com
Swedish Open Cultural Heritage
  ksamsok.se
The National Archives, UK
  nationalarchives.gov.uk
Trove
  trove.nla.gov.au
Trove knitting patterns
  shrouded-ocean-2009.herokuapp.com/patterns
UK Science Museum Group
  sciencemuseumgroup.org.uk
University of British Columbia Open Collection
  open.library.ubc.ca
Vizgu
  vizgu.com
Wikipedia
  wikipedia.org

Appendix B: Introduction to coding

One of the first lessons in learning to code is learning to search the web for examples of code or tutorials matching your needs. In the following I will present the very basics of HTML, CSS, JavaScript, PHP and Python. Where you go from here is up to you. However, I would suggest working through the material provided by the various educational websites for learning web development.

HTML

When I introduce students to web development I always begin with HTML (see more on www.w3.org/html). This is because HTML is the main building block of the web. Even though we now rarely build websites from scratch in HTML, it is still used in conjunction with other web development languages as you will see in the examples of Chapters 5 and 6.

The acronym stands for Hyper Text Markup Language, describing a markup language for web documents. HTML was developed in the late 1980s and early 1990s by Tim Berners-Lee. It is based on the Standard Generalised Markup Language (SGML), from which the concept of tag pairs comes. Both are used to mark up structural units (e.g. paragraphs, headings, list items, etc.). In this way the documents that are marked up can be displayed on any machine (Raggett, 1998). HTML consists of pre-defined elements (tag pairs or single tags) which determine how the content between the tags is presented in any browser. For example, the header tags '<h1> … </h1>' always represent the topmost header, and is by default always styled as the largest of the headers on a webpage; while the single tag '<br/>', by default renders a line break.

In HTML, comments begin with <!— and finish with —>.

The basic example below illustrates the following HTML code:

- a declaration that the document is HTML;
- the <html> root tags enveloping the page;
- the <head> tags enveloping the metadata about the document;
- the <title> tags specifying the title of the page – displayed in the browser window;
- the <body> tags enveloping the visible page content;
- the <h1> tags defining the top heading;
- the <p> tags defining a paragraph.

```
<!DOCTYPE html>
<html>
 <head>
 <title>My Title</title>
 </head>
 <body>
<!- This is my first comment -->
 <h1>Top heading</h1>
 <p>Hello world!</p>
 </body>
</html>
```

Now search the web for 'learn HTML' to try out tutorials, exercises and reference material on the latest version of HTML.

CSS

While all web browsers understand and are able to render HTML code, the web would be a dull place indeed without Cascading Style Sheets (CSS) (see w3.org/Style/CSS). Imagine if all websites were displayed in the same way, with the same fonts and text size, the same blank background, depending on the choices of the browser. Instead, CSS, proposed by Håkon Wium Lie in 1994, allow web developers to determine specific colours, shapes and sizes for each HTML element.

CSS code can be declared in an HTML document (within a <style> tag pair) or in a separate document to which several HTML documents link. The CSS syntax is made up of a selector (e.g. h1) and declaration sets made up of properties and values in curly brackets, as in:

Selector { Property: Value; Property: Value; }

```
h1 { color: blue; font-size: small;}
```

In CSS comments begin with /* and finish with */

```
<!DOCTYPE html>
<html>
 <head>
 <title>My Title</title>
<style>
/* My first CSS comment */
 h1 { color: blue; font-size: small; }
 #pink-header { color: pink; }
 </style>
 </head>
 <body>
 <h1>First top heading</h1>
 <p>Hello world!</p>
 <h1 id='pink-header'>Second top heading</h1>
 <p>Hello again world!</p>
 </body>
 </html>
```

The example above illustrates how HTML is styled with CSS.

A style is determined for all <h1> tags, rendering the content blue and small on the screen.

Another style determines that any tag with the attribute id='pink-header' must be rendered pink.

The result is that the first top header is rendered blue and small and the second top header is rendered pink and small. This is because the second top header inherits the size from the h1 element but changes the colour because the id attribute is specific to this tag.

One way to test how a combination of CSS and HTML will look in a browser is to run it through an online tester. Search the web for 'test css and html' to see what options are available. Try copying and pasting the code in the example above into the tester to see what happens.

JavaScript

JavaScript is a scripting language developed in 1995 by Brendan Eich for Netscape. It is now widely used in most websites, most notably because of its ability to load new content or connect with servers without reloading the page. This is the technology we have come to know through live search (where suggestions appear while you type) or on maps (where you can navigate and interact seamlessly with the locations). One could say that where HTML defines the content of a web page and CSS specifies the layout and style, JavaScript determines the behaviour (W3Schools.com, 2019a).

JavaScript is written as statements (separated by semicolons) that can be inserted into the head or body of an HTML document enclosed by the

'<script>' tags. Comments begin with // and end with a new line.
Here are some example of such statements:

```
// declaring a variable called x
var x;

// adding a value to the variable
x = 11;

// computing a new variable called y, which is based on x
var y = 5 + x; // the result of y is 16

// a function called "greeting" which takes the values of a and b and
returns them with a space between
function greeting (a, b) {
  return a + " " + b;
}

// now call the function with some text and add the result to the variable z
var z = myFunction("Hello", "World"); // the result of z is "Hello World"
```

You can test these statements and make your own by searching online for 'test javascript online'. You can also find many JavaScript tutorials for beginners and upwards. JavaScript is mainly used in Chapters 5 and 6 to create maps (using openlayers.org and openstreetmap.org) and charts (using chartist.js).

JSON

JavaScript Object Notification (JSON) is a light-weight data-interchange format based on JavaScript, but otherwise it is language independent. JSON is built on collections of name/value pairs (i.e. objects in curly brackets) and lists of values (i.e. arrays in square brackets) (json.org). These objects and arrays can be nested inside each other and the values contained in them are extracted through a path (an array index begins with 0). You can use a JSON beautifier (search online) to get an overview of a JSON dataset and to find the appropriate path.

Here is an example of a JSON dataset and the paths to certain values:

```
{
"artists":[
  {"name":"Anna Ancher", "death":1935},
  {"name":"Marie Krøyer", "death":1940},
  {"name":"Anne Marie Carl Nielsen", "death":1945}
]
}
```

The path for the death of the first artist is:
artist > 0 > death

The path for the name of the third artist is:
   artist > 2 > name

PHP

PHP: Hypertext Preprocessor is an open-source scripting language especially suited for web development (php.net). It was designed by Rasmus Lerdorf in 1994 and has developed organically into a programming language.

PHP script is executed on the server and therefore you must have a web host with PHP (most if not all web hosts include this) or install a webserver on your own computer with PHP (W3Schools.com, 2019b). On the server PHP scripts can be used to access and manipulate databases and other files, send and receive cookies, collect data from forms and much more.

PHP code is enveloped by <?php and ?> and comments can be written in blocks (surrounded by /* and */) or inline using // or #. PHP variables begin with $ and statements end with a semicolon.

Here are some example of such statements:

```php
<?php
/* first we declare
the variable $x and use it to
calculate the variable $y */

$x = 6;
$y = $x + 7; // the result is 13

# we can use PHP to print the result as a HTML top level header
echo "<h1>" . $y . "</h1>";

// we can create an array of artists
$artists = array("Anna", "Marie", "Anne");

// and use the foreach loop to display each artist with a line-break after
foreach ($artists as $person) {
 echo '$person <br>';
}

// we can create a function to call a particular artist from the array
function callArtist($i) {
 $artists = array("Anna", "Marie", "Anne");
 echo "Hi $artists[$i]";
}

// and execute the function with the second person (array index = 1)
callArtist(1); // result is "Hi Marie"

?>
```

Try testing this code in an online environment (search for 'test php online') and work through some of the many PHP tutorials available on the web.

Python

Python is a general-purpose open source programming language developed by Guido van Rossum in the 1980s. It was first released in 1991 and is described as fast, friendly and easy to learn (python.org). Python can be used for a variety of developments including desktop applications, websites, games, etc. It is widely used for data science because of its data manipulation tools and its relatively gentle learning curve.

In order to develop with Python you will need to have it installed or access an online environment (search 'online python'). However, most PCs and Macs will have it installed and it can be run from the Terminal or Command Line (W3Schools.com, 2019c).

Python uses indentation to specify a block of code and therefore there are no other indications that a code is ready to execute. Variables in Python do not need to be declared and have no prefix, and comments begin with a hashtag.

Here are some examples of Python code:

```
# first we define two variables, calculate a third and print the result (11)
x = 3
y = 8
z = x + y
print(z)

# print the data type of the x variable, result is int
print(type(x))

# create a list of artists
artist = ["Anna", "Marie", "Anne"]

# make a for loop and print each of the values in the list
for x in artist:
 print(x)
```

Test this Python code by running Python in Terminal (Mac) or Command Line (PC) (W3Schools.com, 2019c) and input the code line by line. Press enter to execute each line.

References

Adams, M. O. (2007) Analyzing Archives and Finding Facts: use and users of digital data records, *Archival Science*, 7 (1), 21–36, https://doi.org/10.1007/s10502-007-9056-4.

Agarwal, M. (2017) Pythonic Data Cleaning with Pandas and NumPy, *Real Python* (blog), https://realpython.com/python-data-cleaning-numpy-pandas/#comment-3840504040.

Arab Image Foundation (2019) *Image Use Guidelines*, http://arabimagefoundation.com/getEntityFront?page=PageDetails&entity-Name=PageEntity&idEntity=11.

Archives Nationales (2018) *Les Archives nationales font leur hackathon*, http://www.archives-nationales.culture.gouv.fr/les-archives-nationales-font-leur-hackathon.

Austen, J. (1813) *Pride and Prejudice*, T. Egerton.

Bekendtgørelse Af Arkivloven (2016) https://www.retsinformation.dk/forms/r0710.aspx?id=183862.

Bekendtgørelse Af Lov Om Ophavsret (2014) https://www.retsinformation.dk/Forms/R0710.aspx?id=164796.

Bekendtgørelse Af Museumsloven (2014) https://www.retsinformation.dk/forms/r0710.aspx?id=162504.

Bennett, T. (1995) *The Birth of the Museum: history, theory, politics*, http://www.123library.org/book_details/?id=112588.

Berners-Lee, T. (2009) Linked Data, *W3C* (blog), (18 June), http://www.w3.org/DesignIssues/LinkedData.html.

Cornish, G. P. (2015) *Copyright: interpreting the law for libraries, archives and information services*, Facet Publishing, http://public.eblib.com/choice/publicfullrecord.aspx?p=2073251.

Cornwell, T. (2019) Arab Photography Archive Releases 22,000 Historic Images Online, (30 May), https://www.theartnewspaper.com/news/arab-photography-archive-releases-22-000-historic-images-online.

Crawford, G. (2009) Amateur and Amateurism. In Blackshaw, T. and Crawford, G. (eds), *The SAGE Dictionary of Leisure Studies*, SAGE.

Creative Commons (2011) History, *CC Wiki* (blog), https://wiki.creativecommons.org/wiki/History.

—— (2019a) *Frequently Asked Questions*, https://creativecommons.org/faq/ #what-is-creative-commons-and-what-do-you-do.

—— (2019b) *Understanding Free Cultural Works*, https://creativecommons.org/share-your-work/public-domain/freeworks/.

De Groot, J. (2009) *Consuming History: Historians and Heritage in Contemporary Popular Culture*, Routledge.

Det Kongelige Bibliotek (2019) *About Netarchive*, http://netarkivet.dk/in-english/.

DigiCULT (2003) *Europe: creating cooperation for digitization*, https://web.archive.org/web/20060626233317/https://cordis.europa.eu/ist/ka3/ digicult/eeurope-overview.htm, https://cordis.europa.eu/ist/ka3/digicult/ eeurope-overview.htm.

Dombrowski, Q. (2010) Codex Assemanius, *Flickr* (blog), https://www.flickr.com/photos/quinnanya/albums/72157624174875338/.

DPLA (2019) *DPLA Developer Resources*, https://dp.la/guides/guide?guide=for-developers.

Dungey, A. M. and Black, J. (2013) *Ask a Slave*, http://www.askaslave.com.

Elings, M. W. and Waibel, G. (2007) Metadata for All: descriptive standards and metadata sharing across libraries, archives and museums, *First Monday*, **12** (3), https://uncommonculture.org/ojs/index.php/fm/article/view/1628/1543.

Ellis, C., Adams, T. E. and Bochner, A. P. (2011) Autoethnography: an overview, *Forum Qualitative Sozialforschung / Forum: Qualitative Social Research*, 12 (1).

European Commission (2019) *H2020 Online Manual*, https://ec.europa.eu/research/participants/docs/h2020-funding-guide/ index_en.htm.

European Union (2016) *General Data Protection Regulation*, https://eur-lex.europa. eu/legal-content/EN/TXT/HTML/?uri=CELEX:32016R0679&from=EN.

Europeana (2015) *The Data Exchange Agreement*, (19 February), https://pro.europeana.eu/page/the-data-exchange-agreement.

—— (2016) Europeana Colour Explorer, *Europeana Pro* (blog), (2 November), https://pro.europeana.eu/data/europeana-colour-explorer.

Fitzgerald, B., Shi, S. X., Foong, C. and Pappalardo, K. (2015) Country of Origin and Internet Publication: applying the Berne Convention in the digital age. In Fitzgerald, B. and Gilchrist, J. (eds), *Copyright Perspectives: Past, Present and Prospect*, Springer International Publishing, https://doi.org/10.1007/978-3-319-15913-3_4.

Freedom Defined (2015) Definition, *Definition of Free Cultural Works* (blog), https://freedomdefined.org/Definition.

—— (2017) Licenses/NC, *Definition of Free Cultural Works* (blog), https://freedomdefined.org/Licenses/NC.

Gandhi Heritage Portal (2019) *Chronology: event detail page,* https://www.gandhiheritageportal.org/eventcontentdetail/OA==/NzQxOQ==.

Grahame-Smith, S. and Austen, J. (2009) *Pride and Prejudice and Zombies: the classic Regency romance – now with ultraviolent zombie mayhem,* Quirk Classics, Quirk Books.

Hackathon Bandung (2018) *Why a Hackathon on Bandung's Heritage?* https://web.archive.org/web/20190528143217/http:/hackathonbandung.com/concept/.

Hamilton, G. and Saunderson, F. (2017) *Open Licensing for Cultural Heritage,* Facet Publishing.

Hill, K. (2016) *Women and Museums 1850–1914: modernity and the gendering of knowledge,* Oxford University Press.

Højsgaard, L. (2018) Arkiver sætter lid til GDPR-pragmatisme, *DM Natur & Kultur* (blog), (December), https://dm.dk/sektorer-i-dm/dm-viden/landsklubben-for-forskning-og-formidling/magasinet-dm-natur-kultur/dm-natur-kultur-2018/lkffdecember2018/05-arkiver-saetter-lid-til-gdpr-pragmatisme.

Howard, P. (2003) *Heritage: management, interpretation, identity,* Continuum.

Hughes, L. M. (2004) *Digitizing Collections: strategic issues for the information manager,* Digital Futures Series, Facet Publishing.

Internet Archive (2019) *About the Internet Archive,* https://archive.org/about/.

Jurczyk-Romanowska, E. and Tufekčić, A. (2018) The Development of Genealogy in Europe, Based on the Examples of Poland, Italy, Turkey and Bosnia and Herzegovina, *European Journal of Education,* 1 (3), 177–93.

Kelly, K., Council on Library and Information Resources and Andrew W. Mellon Foundation (2013) *Images of Works of Art in Museum Collections: The Experience of Open Access: A Study of 11 Museums,* https://www.clir.org/pubs/reports/pub157/.

Kolding Stadsarkiv (2019) *Kolding Stadsarkiv: Strategi- og Handleplan 2019–2022.*

Labrador, A. M. and Chilton, E. S. (2009) Re-locating Meaning in Heritage Archives: a call for participatory heritage databases, *Computer Applications to Archaeology: Williamsburg, VA, 22–26 March,* https://works.bepress.com/angela_labrador/5/.

Levine, P. (1986) *The Amateur and the Professional: antiquarians, historians and archaeologists in Victorian England, 1838–1886,* Cambridge University Press.

Levy, S. (1984) *Hackers: heroes of the computer Revolution,* 1st edn, Anchor Press/Doubleday.

Lifshitz-Goldberg, Y. (2010) Orphan Works. In https://www.wipo.int/edocs/mdocs/sme/en/wipo_smes_ge_10/wipo_smes_ge_10_ref_theme11_02.pdf.

Lorentzen, R., Nielsen, J. F., Madsen, H. B. and Gjelstrup, M. (2015) Mærk Historien, presented at the *Hack4DK, DR,* https://drive.google.com/file/d/0B9yZllJxryfpZVRXcV9MVUtPYlU/view.

McCarthy, D. (2019) Licensing Policy and Practice in Open GLAM, *Medium* (blog), (16 April), https://medium.com/open-glam/licensing-policy-and-practice-in-open-glam-49c867b49de8.

McCarthy, D. and Wallace, A. (2019) *Survey of GLAM Open Access Policy and Practice*, https://docs.google.com/spreadsheets/d/1WPS-KJptUJ-o8SXtg00llcxq0IKJu8eO6Ege_GrLaNc/edit#gid=1216556120.

Natural History Museum, London (2018) When Sir David Attenborough Meets Himself in Virtual Reality, *Facebook*, https://www.facebook.com/naturalhistorymuseum/videos/10155209172166537/.

Obama, B. (2013) *Executive Order – making open and machine readable the new default for government information*, (5 September), https://obamawhitehouse.archives.gov/the-press-office/2013/05/09/executive-order-making-open-and-machine-readable-new-default-government-.

Olsen, H. R. (2005) Poul Helweg Mikkelsen – en Amatørarkæolog: Amatorarkæologi I 1930'erne På Holsted-Egnen, *Mark Og Montre: Årbog for Ribe Amts Museer*, 41.

Open Knowledge International (2019a) Open Definition 2.1, *Open Definition* (blog), http://opendefinition.org.

—— (2019b) What Is Open Data? *Open Data Handbook* (blog), http://opendatahandbook.org/guide/en/what-is-open-data/.

OpenGLAM (2019) *OpenGLAM Principles*, https://openglam.org/principles/.

Oxford Living Dictionaries (2020) Oxford Dictionaries | English, https://en.oxforddictionaries.com/definition/amateur.

Padfield, T. (2015) *Copyright for Archivists and Records Managers*, 5th rev. edn, Facet Publishing.

Pekel, J. (2014) *Democratising the Rijksmuseum*, https://pro.europeana.eu/files/Europeana_Professional/Publications/Democratising%20the%20Rijksmuseum.pdf.

Petri, G. (2014) The Public Domain vs. the Museum: the limits of copyright and reproductions of two-dimensional works of art, *Journal of Conservation and Museum Studies*, 12 (1), https://doi.org/10.5334/jcms.1021217.

Post & Tele Museum (n.d.) Katalog, http://frimaerker.ptt-museum.dk/katalog/1.

Raggett, D. (1998) A History of HTML. In *Raggett on HTML 4*, https://www.w3.org/People/Raggett/book4/ch02.html.

Rayner, T. (2018) *Hacker Culture and the New Rules of Innovation*, Routledge.

Ridge, M. (2017) The Contributions of Family and Local Historians to British History Online. In Roued-Cunliffe, H. and Copeland, A. J. (eds), *Participatory Heritage*, Facet Publishing.

Rijksmuseum (2019a) *Create Your Own Route*, https://www.rijksmuseum.nl/en/create-your-own-route.

—— (2019b) *Everything about the Rijksstudio Award 2020*, https://www.rijksmuseum.nl/en/rijksstudioaward.

Rosati, E. (2017) The Monkey Selfie Case and the Concept of Authorship: an EU perspective, *Journal of Intellectual Property Law & Practice*, 12 (12), 973–77, https://doi.org/10.1093/jiplp/jpx199.

Rosenzweig, R. (2006) Can History Be Open Source? Wikipedia and the future of the past, *Journal of American History*, 93 (1), 117–46, https://doi.org/10.2307/4486062.

Roued-Cunliffe, H. (2017) Forgotten History on Wikipedia. In Roued-Cunliffe, H. and Copeland, A. J. (eds), *Participatory Heritage*, Facet Publishing.

—— (2018) Developing Sustainable Open Heritage Datasets. In Levenberg, L., Neilson, T. and Rheams, D. (eds), *Research Methods for the Digital Humanities*, Springer, https://link-springer-com.ep.fjernadgang.kb.dk/content/pdf/10.1007%2F978-3-319-96713-4_16.pdf.

Roued Olsen, H. (2007a) *Heritage Portals and Cross-Border Data Interoperability*, MSc thesis, University of Southampton.

—— (2007b) Reflections on Culture Connections – examining connections between South Scandinavia and the Sîntana de Mures/Çernjachov Culture from AD 270–410 (Period C2 to D1), *LAG*, 8.

Royal Armouries (2019) History of the Royal Armouries in the Tower of London, https://royalarmouries.org/about-us/history-of-the-royal-armouries/history-of-the-royal-armouries-in-the-tower-of-london/.

Ruge, C., Denison, D., Wright, S., Willett, G. and Evans, J. (2017) Custodianship and Online Sharing in Australian Community Archives. In Roued-Cunliffe, H. and Copeland, A. J. (eds), *Participatory Heritage*, Facet Publishing.

Samoilenko, A., Lemmerich, F., Weller, K., Zens, M. and Strohmaier, M. (2017) Analysing Timelines of National Histories across Wikipedia Editions: a comparative computational approach, *ArXiv:1705.08816 [Cs]*, May, http://arxiv.org/abs/1705.08816.

Sanderhoff, M. (2017) Small Steps, Big Impact: how SMK became SMK Open. In Hamilton, G. and Saunderson, F. (eds), *Open Licensing for Cultural Heritage*, Facet Publishing.

Sang-Hun, C., Hanley, C. J. and Mendoz, M. (1999) War's Hidden Chapter: ex-GIs tell of killing Korean refugees, *Associated Press*, (29 September).

Savolainen, R. (1995) Everyday Life Information Seeking: approaching information seeking in the context of 'way of life', *Library and Information Science Research*, 17 (3), 259–94.

Schudel, M. (2006) Henriette Avram, 'Mother of MARC,' Dies, *Information Bulletin*, May, https://www.loc.gov/loc/lcib/0605/avram.html.

Science Group Museum (2019) Using Our Collection API, https://www.sciencemuseumgroup.org.uk/about-us/collection/using-our-collection-api/.

Sherratt, T. (2019a) Visualise Trove Newspaper Searches over Time, *Jupyter Nbviewer* (blog), https://nbviewer.jupyter.org/github/GLAM-Workbench/trove-newspapers/blob/master/visualise-searches-over-time.ipynb#9.-But-what-are-we-searching.

—— (2019b) Trove: connecting us to the past, *Tim Sherratt* (blog), (6 July), https://timsherratt.org/blog/trove-connecting-us/.

Sinn, D. (2017) No Gun Ri Digital Archive: challenges in archiving memory for a historically marginalized incident. In Roued-Cunliffe, H. and Copeland, A. J. (eds), *Participatory Heritage*, Facet Publishing.

Skov, M. (2013) Hobby-related Information-seeking Behaviour of Highly Dedicated Online Museum Visitors, *Information Research*, 18 (4), www.informationr.net/ir/18-4/paper597.html#.U_B7fUhDLw0.

Smith, J. H. (2017) Instant SMK Art Info? There's an app for that, *Medium* (blog), (8 April), https://medium.com/smk-open/instant-smk-art-info-theres-an-app-for-that-81a836e17eed.

Smithsonian (2019) *Terms of Use*, https://www.si.edu/termsofuse.

South Dublin County Council (2018) *South Dublin Heritage Walks*, https://web.archive.org/web/20180729224503/http://heritagewalks.sdcc.ie.

Stebbins, R. A. (1979) *Amateurs: On the margin between work and leisure*, Sage. http://www.seriousleisure.net/uploads/8/3/3/8/8338986/amateurs.pdf.

Stebbins, R. A. (2007) *Serious Leisure: a perspective for our time*, Transaction Publishers.

Su, B. (2012) *The Lizzie Bennet Diaries*, https://www.youtube.com/channel/UCXfbQAimgtbk4RAUHtIAUww.

Terras, M. (2011) The Rise of Digitization. In Rikowski, R. (ed.), *Digitisation Perspectives*, SensePublishers, https://doi.org/10.1007/978-94-6091-299-3.

—— (2014) Reuse of Digitised Content (4): chasing an orphan work through the UK's new copyright licensing scheme, *Melissa Terras* (blog), (29 October), https://melissaterras.org/2014/10/29/reuse-of-digitised-content-4-chasing-an-orphan-work-through-the-uks-new-copyright-licensing-scheme/.

—— (2015a) Cultural Heritage Information: artefacts and digitization technologies. In Ruthven, I. and Chowdhury, G. G. (eds),*Cultural Heritage Information: access and management*, Facet Publishing.

—— (2015b) Opening Access to Collections: the making and using of open digitised cultural content, ed. G. E. Gorman and P. Jennifer, *Online Information Review*, 39 (5), 733–52, https://doi.org/10.1108/OIR-06-2015-0193.

The National Archives (2018) *Guide to Archiving Personal Data*, www.nationalarchives.gov.uk/documents/information-management/guide-to-archiving-personal-data.pdf.

Trove (2019a) API Overview, *Trove Help Centre* (blog), https://help.nla.gov.au/trove/building-with-trove/api.

—— (2019b) Trove API Survey Appendix A: examples of websites and apps, *Trove Help Centre* (blog), https://help.nla.gov.au/trove/api-overview/trove-api-survey-appendix-examples-of-websites-and-apps.

UNESCO (1972) *Convention Concerning the Protection of the World Cultural and Natural Heritage*, https://whc.unesco.org/en/conventiontext/.

—— (2003) *Convention for the Safeguarding of the Intangible Cultural Heritage*, https://ich.unesco.org/doc/src/2003_Convention_Basic_Texts-_2018_ version-EN.pdf.

—— (2008) *World Heritage Information Kit*, https://whc.unesco.org/document/102072.

—— (2019) *UNESCO Database of National Cultural Heritage Laws*, https://en.unesco.org/cultnatlaws.

UNESCO ICH (2018) *Operational Directives for the Implementation of the Convention for the Safeguarding of the Intangible Heritage*, https://ich.unesco.org/doc/src/ICH-Operational_Directives-7.GA-PDF-EN.pdf.

—— (2019) *Frequently Asked Questions*, https://ich.unesco.org/en/faq-00021.

Verwayen, H. (2017) *An Impact Playbook for Cultural Heritage? This ain't gonna be easy, Europeana Pro*, https://pro.europeana.eu/post/an-impact-playbook-for-cultural-heritage-this-ain-t-gonna-be-easy.

W3C (2015), *Semantic Web*, https://www.w3.org/standards/semanticweb/.

W3Schools.com (2019a) *JavaScript Tutorial*, https://www.w3schools.com/js/default.asp.

—— (2019b) *PHP Installation*, https://www.w3schools.com/php/php_install.asp.

—— (2019c) *Python Getting Started*, https://www.w3schools.com/python/python_getstarted.asp.

Welland, F. (2008) The History of Jane Austen's Writing Desk, *Persuasions*, 30, 125–8.

Wikipedia (2019a) List of Countries' Copyright Lengths, *Wikipedia* (blog), https://en.wikipedia.org/wiki/List_of_countries%27_copyright_lengths.

—— (2019b) *Wikipedia: GLAM/About*, https://en.wikipedia.org/wiki/Wikipedia:GLAM/About.

—— (2019c) *Wikipedia: GLAM/The Children's Museum of Indianapolis*, https://en.wikipedia.org/wiki/Wikipedia:GLAM/The_Children%27s_ Museum_of_Indianapolis.

WIPO (1886) *Berne Convention for the Protection of Literary and Artistic Works*, https://www.wipo.int/treaties/en/ip/berne/summary_berne.html.

Wright, E., Viner-Daniels, S., Albarella, U., Street, M., Makowiecki, D., Steppan, K. and Brugal, J.-P. (2016) Biometrical Database of European Aurochs and Domestic Cattle, ed. E. Wright, *Open Context*, http://doi.org/10.6078/M7TX3C9V.

Index